AGREEMENT
ON BERLIN

AEI-Hoover
policy studies

The studies in this series are issued jointly
by the American Enterprise Institute
for Public Policy Research and the Hoover
Institution on War, Revolution and Peace.
They are designed to focus on
policy problems of current and future interest,
to set forth the factors underlying
these problems and to evaluate
courses of action available to policymakers.
The views expressed in these studies
are those of the authors and do not necessarily
reflect the views of the staff, officers
or members of the governing boards of
AEI or the Hoover Institution.

AGREEMENT ON BERLIN

A study of the 1970-72 quadripartite negotiations

Dennis L. Bark

American Enterprise Institute for Public Policy Research
Washington, D.C.

Hoover Institution on War, Revolution and Peace
Stanford University, Stanford, California

AEI-Hoover Policy Study 10, August 1974
(Hoover Institution Studies 45)

ISBN 0-8447-3135-8

Library of Congress Catalog Card No. 74-83507

Printed in United States of America

For
Peter-Carl
and
Robert Mark

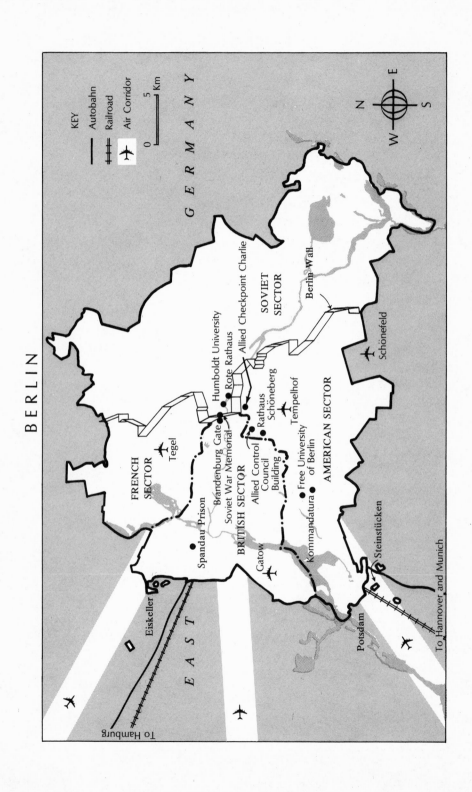

BERLIN

G E R M A N Y

E A S T

KEY
— Autobahn
╫╫╫ Railroad
✈ Air Corridor

0   5
╟━━━┥ Km

N
W ✦ E
S

To Hamburg

Eiskeller

Spandau Prison

Tegel ✈

FRENCH SECTOR

Gatow ✈

BRITISH SECTOR

Brandenburg Gate
Soviet War Memorial

Humboldt University
Rote Rathaus

Allied Checkpoint Charlie

SOVIET SECTOR

Berlin Wall

Allied Control
Council Building

Rathaus Schöneberg

Tempelhof

Free University of Berlin

Kommandatura

AMERICAN SECTOR

Schönefeld ✈

Steinstücken

Potsdam

✈

To Hannover and Munich

Contents

Introduction

Berlin, a "cosmopolitan crossroads of Europe" and not too long ago the capital of the most powerful state in the world, has suffered since 1939 as no other great city has suffered. Treated as a pawn in the political chess game between rival forces of East and West, it has been made captive in its now divided homeland. Disputes over its status have on occasion brought the world to the brink of war. The essence of the humiliation of this proud and beautiful metropolis has been that though its citizens had the most to lose in its struggle for freedom, they have had the least to say about its destiny.

With painful deliberation, the world powers of West and East began to resolve some of the issues relative to the Berlin question a quarter century after the end of World War II. From 26 March 1970 to 3 September 1971, Great Britain, France, the Soviet Union, and the United States met to negotiate a settlement that would eliminate Berlin as a source of tension in Europe, and that would restore some sense of normality to divided Berlin. It is to be hoped that their agreement, the 1971 Quadripartite Agreement on Berlin, will allow West Berliners to live with greater freedom and dignity and that the rest of the world will also profit from this act of justice.

West Berlin is important for many reasons. It is a city of approximately two million people, and it would of course be important for that reason alone. But there is more to it than this. Germany occupies a crucial position in Europe for two reasons. The first is geographical. The German plains form the gateway between Eastern and Western Europe. Germany has been and will continue to be the key to conventional military security and stability in Europe. The second reason is economic. Each of the two Germanys, West and East, is the premier

1

industrial nation within its respective European orbit. This combination of geography and industrial strength makes the study of Germany important for an understanding of inter-European relations. And if the study of Germany is a key to understanding Europe, the study of Berlin is a key to understanding Germany.

Berlin is a central figure in intra-German relations. The city is located 110 miles inside East Germany. In 1945, for a series of complicated reasons, Berliners living in the twelve boroughs that were to be the Western sectors of occupation found themselves without a guaranteed form of access to the main zones of Western Allied occupation. It is probably true that few believed that the wartime division of Germany would be permanent. But as the years went by, the division of Germany and the division of Berlin became progressively more firmly established.

By any standards the question of Berlin has presented enormously complex problems. The Western sectors were governed by democratic procedures but located in the heart of the Soviet zone of influence. The Soviet Union and East Germany, in order to protest West Berlin's existence or to call attention to any activity going on within West Berlin, could sever land routes to the city at any time. Land access, or the lack of it, was a key to the political situation in 1970 before the Berlin negotiations began.

West Berliners are justly proud of their city. After the war and after their economic recovery, they were determined that West Berlin should not be reduced to a military bastion. Berlin and its traditions were to live, and so was the freedom of twelve of its twenty boroughs. For the city to live, it had to have adequate access ways. The hustle and the bustle of an exciting city consists of more than just the movement of the city's own inhabitants within its borders. It also consists of visitors, businessmen, students, professors and tourists coming in and going out of the city. And the city's businesses need a continual flow of goods to operate. Airplanes, despite improvements since the Berlin blockade in 1948, are not large enough carriers to keep a city alive commercially. West Berliners needed a guaranteed form of land access to their city—road, rail and water—which would permit the movement of bulk goods, large numbers of travelers, and all the other things a city needs in order to stay alive.

Access, of course, was not the only difficulty the city faced. Another was that its residents were not in a position to solve West

2

Berlin's problems themselves. West Berlin became a focal point for the cold war—not because West Berlin was in any sense the cause of the cold war or because it contributed to it, but because at any given time the temperature of the cold war could be measured by the tensions in Berlin. In a sense, West Berliners were hostages. Their city was so positioned that whenever the Soviet Union or the government of East Germany objected to a Western action, a visible and painful protest could be lodged by harassing the autobahns, railroads or canals leading to West Berlin.

Germany, it should be noted, has not signed a formal treaty ending the Second World War. As one result, it is the four powers—Great Britain, France, the Soviet Union, and the United States—and not East and West Germany—that are still legally responsible for Greater Berlin. The two Germanys, even if they desired, could not legally negotiate a settlement of the Berlin problem on their own.

Here a qualification is required. By 1970, East and West Germany obviously could have held meetings on their own to establish measures which would improve life for the West Berliners. But they could not determine the city's status. While the formal military occupation of Germany was ended in the early 1950s, the formal military occupation of Berlin continues to exist to the present day. East Germany was so closely tied to the Soviet Union, however, and West Germany to Britain, France and the United States, that it would have been unlikely that either would have moved independently of its allies' wishes. In this way Berlin, and in particular West Berlin, became a pawn in the cold war.

Just as the two German governments could not be entirely independent of their allies, their allies could not act without consideration for German wishes. West Germany had slowly been moving on its own toward an easing of as many tensions with the East as was possible and practical. Chancellor Kiesinger's government (1966-1969) began its own initiatives in 1967. Willy Brandt, who became chancellor in 1969, accelerated the process. One of his major desires, certainly, was to ease the Berlin situation.

Brandt was not alone in his efforts to ease tension in Europe. In 1969 Richard Nixon, soon after his election as President of the United States, undertook a series of initiatives which would contribute to a new process of détente, meaning deliberate attempts to ease existing tension through negotiation. This was the policy which the United States government carefully began to pursue.

The first step was the President's visit to the capitals of Western Europe and to Berlin five weeks after his inauguration. Berlin had been a source of recurrent tension in Europe for two decades and was a problem which required solution. It is difficult to explain exactly what the Eastern European nations expected of the Berlin negotiations. But certainly their desires included increased trade and technological help. Another motive was the Soviet Union's interest in an agreement that would give legal status to the World War II division of Europe.

The Soviet Union's desire to legitimize the status quo, however, was feared in West Germany. The West Germans had never wanted to recognize the division of Germany as final. One of the two largest parties in West Germany, the Christian Democratic/Christian Socialist (CDU/CSU) bloc, was determined that neither the Western Allies nor the West German government would approve steps which could be interpreted as agreement to legitimize and to perpetuate the country's division. But West German opinion was divided on what those steps might be. While a large number of West German citizens were no longer sure that it was worth even trying to maintain the legal idea of one Germany, there was an equally large number who questioned whether détente was possible at all.

The Berlin situation, then, was a complicated one with at least seven parties interested in its solution—East Germany, West Germany, the West Berliners, the Soviet Union, the United States, Great Britain, and France. Many saw the 1970-1971 quadripartite negotiations on Berlin as a test of détente. How close together had the Eastern and Western nations come? Could political tensions in Europe be reduced? Would negotiations produce viable and mutually acceptable agreements?

This book will focus specifically upon the Berlin negotiations in an effort to adopt to some extent a West Berliner's point of view. To explain the negotiations and what they represented, a chronological case-book approach to the development of the West German position on these negotiations has been chosen. It is hoped that this approach will help to make clear what the negotiations accomplished and what they failed to accomplish and, in addition, will provide insight into future and continuing problems. And there are such problems. For example, it was clear when the agreement was signed that the issue of a West German federal presence in West Berlin had not been completely settled.

Diplomatic negotiations in modern as well as past times are generally long and drawn out. The quadripartite negotiations on Berlin were no exception. The ambassadors (the negotiator for each country had the rank of ambassador) met once or twice a month for eighteen months before they were able to agree upon a document. Even after they had the document, it took an additional nine months to work out the details so that the agreement could be enacted. While West Germany did not have an active diplomatic role in the negotiations, its government and the West German press followed them closely. In the negotiations, West Germany had to consider what it would allow the three Western powers to use as possible bargaining counters. What claims was it willing to relinquish? What was it willing to concede to East Germany and the Soviet Union? How would concessions affect the future of the two Germanys and the future of West Berlin?

In a wider context the debates within West Germany were representative of concerns felt within other capitals about détente and the development of East-West relations as a whole. Willy Brandt was a minority chancellor with a slim margin of votes in the Bundestag (lower house of the federal legislature; the upper house is the Bundesrat). He had to be concerned with criticism from his opposition, and with Western criticism as well. West Germany and West Berlin had to live with and deal with the problems arising from the Berlin situation without having a direct role in the negotiations to solve those problems. But their consent was necessary for a solution. In the end, their consent was given. It is important to see how this came about, not only because their consent was necessary, but also because the process by which it came to be given will tell us something about the general nature of the Berlin problem.

1

The Experience of Past Agreements:
1944 through 1969

West German positions on the 1970-71 negotiations were not formed in a vacuum. Since 1945, Berlin had been governed under the 1944-45 quadripartite agreements dividing the city into sectors and the 1949 quadripartite agreement ending the blockade. To understand West German positions during the 1970-71 negotiations, it is important to understand how previous agreements affected Berlin's development.

The continuing right of quadripartite occupation and administration was a central question. The United States, Great Britain and France justified their presence in Berlin on the basis of the 1944-45 and 1949 agreements. It was not, of course, the validity of the past agreements alone that permitted the Western powers to protect the citizens of Berlin; it was that validity coupled with their resolve to remain in the city despite Soviet efforts to force their withdrawal. These agreements could not be unilaterally terminated by any of the four signatories—Great Britain, France, the Soviet Union, or the United States—or by any unilateral declaration by a fifth party, such as the government of the German Democratic Republic (East Germany, or GDR) or of the Federal Republic of Germany (West Germany). Nor could events like the building of the Berlin Wall invalidate these agreements. To be sure, over the years each side had developed its own interpretation of its rights in Berlin, and by 1970 it had become difficult to separate actual quadripartite rights from asserted ones.

The Quadripartite Agreements of 1944-45

In London, on 12 September and 14 November 1944, the members of the European Advisory Commission [1]—Great Britain, the United States,

---

[1] For a description of the origins of the European Advisory Commission, its representatives, and its activity see Lord William Strang, *Home and Abroad* (London: A. Deutsch, 1956).

and the Soviet Union—concluded two important accords. These accords defined the status of the Berlin area, which was to be occupied by troops of the three victorious powers although it was within territory designated as the Soviet zone of occupation. The protocol of 12 September 1944 provided for the occupation and division of Germany into three zones, and for "a special Berlin area, which will be under joint occupation by the three Powers." As with the occupation zones themselves, the "special Berlin area" was clearly marked on the map included as Annex B to the protocol. In the protocol the "special Berlin area" was defined as "Greater Berlin." It was to be divided into three sectors to be occupied by the forces of Great Britain, the United States, and the Soviet Union. Provision was made for an "Inter-Allied Governing Authority [*Kommandatura*] consisting of three Commandants, appointed by their respective Commanders-in-Chief . . . established to direct jointly the administration of the 'Greater Berlin' area." [2]

The agreement of 14 November 1944 concerned the control machinery for Berlin and Germany. The Kommandatura for Greater Berlin was to operate under the general direction of the Control Council which was created to coordinate the administration of the three original zones of occupation and was to be located in Greater Berlin.[3] In accordance with the Yalta Agreement of February 1945, the accord of 14 November 1944 was amended on 1 May 1945 to provide for the participation of France in the Control Council and in the Inter-Allied Governing Authority. Later, in the four-power agreement of 26 July 1945 (which amended the protocol of 12 September 1944), provision was made for a French zone of occupation and for a French sector in Greater Berlin.

---

[2] The documents and supplementary accords of the 1944 and 1945 quadripartite agreements can be found in U.S. Department of State, *Documents on Germany, 1944-1959* (Washington, D.C.: Government Printing Office, 1959), pp. 1-24. This publication will be hereafter referred to as *Documents, 1944-1959*.

[3] At the Yalta conference Churchill, Roosevelt, and Stalin agreed on the final borders for the division of Germany among the three powers. Maneuvering on who would get which parts of Germany had been taking place since 1943. The Allies were determined that an occupation force would be set up in Germany to destroy all traces of Nazism and militarism in that country, and to make sure that the German armies and General Staff were completely disbanded. The occupation and its work were to be coordinated by the Control Council located in Berlin. Berlin was also divided and that division was entirely separate from the division of Germany. The administration of the city was then to be coordinated by the Kommandatura. It was also at the Yalta conference that the territory east of the Oder-Neisse line was given to Poland.

The "Declaration Regarding the Defeat of Germany and the Assumption of Supreme Authority by the Allied Powers," the "Allied Statement on Zones of Occupation in Germany," and the "Allied Statement on Control Machinery in Germany," all issued on 5 June 1945, declared the assumption of "supreme authority" in Germany and in Berlin by the four Allied powers. In November 1945 and October 1946 agreements were concluded among the four powers establishing the air corridors connecting West Berlin's two civilian airports of Tempelhof and Tegel and the military airport of Gatow with airports in West Germany.

According to the agreements of 1944-45, Greater Berlin was designated as a 'special' area under a separate occupation authority. It did not constitute a part of the Soviet or of any other zone of occupation. The protocols concluded during the Potsdam conference in July and August 1945 concerning joint Allied administration of occupied Germany did not pertain to the administration or occupation of the "special Berlin area." The agreements concerning Greater Berlin were independent of any decisions taken at Potsdam. Nor is the Potsdam Agreement mentioned in any quadripartite accord concluded since 1945. Any claims to the contrary, such as those made by the Soviet and East German governments, are without basis in fact.[4] Assertions by the Soviet and East German governments that ostensible violations of the Potsdam Agreement by England, France, or the United States constituted an abrogation of their rights of occupation in Berlin directly contradict the agreements determining the occupation and administration of Berlin.[5]

The Western Allies' rights in Berlin are of an "original character." That is to say, occupation by the Western Allies of their respective zones in Germany and their respective sectors in Berlin occurred as a result of the defeat of Germany by the Allied powers. Western rights of occupation in Berlin and access to the city do not represent a Soviet concession, but are based on the agreements of 12 September and 14 November 1944. Soviet claims that the right of Western occupation

[4] See Jens Hacker, *Sowjetunion und DDR zum Potsdamer Abkommen* (Cologne: Verlag Wissenschaft und Politik, 1968).

[5] The Soviet Union made this assertion in the "Berlin ultimatum" of 1958. See "Note from the Soviet Foreign Ministry to the American Ambassador at Moscow, regarding Berlin, November 27, 1958," in *Documents, 1944-1959*, pp. 317-331.

of Berlin was granted in exchange for British and American withdrawal from the Soviet zone are assertions without documentary evidence.[6]

These claims have produced considerable argument, especially after the creation of two separate German states in 1949. The Western position was based on the continuing validity of the tripartite and quadripartite agreements on the division and administration of postwar Berlin, agreements to which the Soviet government was a signatory. The Eastern position asserted that the tripartite and quadripartite agreements had been superseded by developments since 1945 and were no longer valid. By the time of the negotiations in 1970, the two positions appeared to be irreconcilable.

Experience with the Agreements: 1945 to 1949

On 1 July 1945, troops of the four powers allied against Germany began to withdraw from the areas they had occupied during the war itself to the respective zones of occupation defined in the London agreements of 1944 and 1945. French troops therefore withdrew from the future "American" zone and American troops from the future "British" zone. American and British troops withdrew from Thuringia, Anhalt, and portions of Mecklenburg and Saxony, all destined to be part of the future "Soviet" zone. With the exception of Greater Berlin, Soviet troops were located only in portions of Germany designated for their occupation. Their movements were therefore limited to occupying the additional territory vacated by Great Britain and the United States. Simultaneously French, British, and American troops occupied the Western sectors of Berlin vacated by the Soviet troops.

The first meeting of the Kommandatura was held in Berlin on 11 July 1945. In Order No. 1, 11 July, the twenty boroughs of Greater Berlin were officially formed into four sectors, each under the jurisdiction of its respective French, British, Soviet, or American commandant. The original division of eight boroughs assigned to the Soviet commandant and six each to the American and British commandants was revised. The Soviet Union retained eight boroughs, including the borough of Stadt-Mitte, in which the offices of the prewar municipal government of Greater Berlin were located. The United States retained

---

[6] Dieter Mahncke, "Verantwortung für Berlin," *Das Ende des Provisoriums, Aussenpolitische Perspektiven des westdeutschen Staates,* vol. 1 (Munich: R. Oldenbourg, 1971), pp. 115-117.

six boroughs and Great Britain allocated two of its six boroughs to France.

Between 1945 and 1948 the municipal government of Berlin, located in the *Rote-Rathaus* (city hall) of Stadt-Mitte, administered the civic affairs of the twenty boroughs of the city. The local government of Greater Berlin was subject to the supreme authority of the four-power Kommandatura.

Quadripartite administration of Greater Berlin gradually deteriorated. A combination of factors including the unanimity requirement for decisions by the Kommandatura, the unresolved disputes of the 1944 and 1945 agreements, the defeat of the Socialist Unity party (SED) in the 1946 elections, and East/West divergence over plans for postwar Germany destroyed any chance that might have existed for four-power cooperation in the administration of the city. Allied cooperation in the Control Council and in the Kommandatura ceased during March and June of 1948, when the Soviet Union withdrew from these bodies on the pretext that the currency reform introduced in West Berlin and West Germany was illegal.[7]

On 24 June 1948 the Soviet Union began a blockade of the land, rail, and water routes connecting the Western sectors of Berlin with the three Western zones of occupation. The actual division of the city followed in November 1948. The partition represented the final step of a program directed by the SED, with Soviet approval, and designed to enable the development of a separate political, economic, and social

---

[7] After the war, West Germany's economic system was in ruin. Inflation had started near the end of the war and then continued during the first years of occupation despite the high taxes imposed by the Allies to try to regulate it. The Reich had left an enormous number of debts outstanding. The Allies did not wish to see the reestablishment of one central German bank. Instead they wanted a diversified system. When discussion started on how the four powers would issue new money that would be needed for a complete currency reform, the Soviet Union demanded that it have a set of printing plates. The United States was determined not to provide a set of plates, however, in view of the experience with the Allied military currency. (The Soviet Union printed the issue as fast as the press could operate, leaving the United States Treasury with the problem of financing it.) By late 1947 each side was at work preparing its own currency and currency reforms. The Western powers introduced their currency reform—which included rules for trading in the old currency for the new, a distribution of the old debts, and the means for a general claims settlement— as a series of measures starting in January and continuing through August 1948. Berlin was not included in the West German currency reform until after the blockade began and after the Soviet Union refused to establish a third currency for the city as a whole. The Soviet government demanded that Russian currency be used in the city.

11

order in the Soviet sector of the city parallel to that being established in the Soviet occupied zone of Germany.

In November 1948, almost five months after the beginning of the blockade and shortly before the municipal elections scheduled for Greater Berlin on 5 December, it appeared that the SED would suffer an even more decisive electoral defeat than it had in 1946. The Soviet Union had three alternatives: (1) the SED could participate in the election and risk almost certain defeat, making effective Soviet control of the city government extremely difficult; (2) the Soviet Union could await possible Western withdrawal from Berlin under pressure of the blockade, leaving the Western sectors subject to its control; or (3) the activity of the legally elected city administration in the Soviet sector could be suppressed by the Soviet commandant. This last alternative could be achieved comparatively easily, since the offices of the municipal government were located in the Soviet sector. Although the municipal government was subject to the decisions of the Kommandatura, the Soviet commandant had unilaterally withdrawn from the Kommandatura in June and he no longer considered its authority to apply to the Soviet sector. This withdrawal was in violation of the agreements of 1944 and 1945 as was the unilateral rejection of the Kommandatura's authority within the Soviet sector.[8]

The crucial turning point for the unity of Berlin occurred on 30 November 1948, six days before the scheduled elections, when the SED created a "provisional democratic magistrate" in the Soviet sector. Soviet sector police forcefully prevented legally elected representatives and officials not sympathetic to the SED, most of whom resided in the Western sectors, from entering their offices in the *Rote-Rathaus*. When Greater Berlin's legally elected mayor, Ferdinand Friedensburg, attempted to enter his office in the Soviet sector on 1 December, he was informed that the newly chosen "mayor" of Berlin, Friedrich Ebert, had issued an order prohibiting the city government from continuing to perform its duties in the Soviet sector.

Thereafter the administrative domain of the legally elected government was confined to the French, British, and American sectors of Berlin. Its offices were reestablished in the American occupied borough of Schöneberg. The Kommandatura continued to hold its regular meetings in the absence of the Soviet commandant, whose chair and

[8] See Elmer Plischke, *Berlin: Development of Its Government and Administration* (Godesberg: Office of the U.S. High Commissioner for Germany, 1952).

offices remained vacant in the Kommandatura building located in the American sector. To this day, the legally elected government of Greater Berlin remains under the supreme authority of the Kommandatura, to which a Soviet commandant could return at any time.

The Berlin Communiqué of 20 June 1949

The success of the Allied airlift forced the Soviet government to terminate the Berlin blockade. In New York City on 4 May 1949 the Soviet Union signed an agreement with the three Western powers according to which the blockade would be lifted on 12 May.[9] At that time the three Western powers agreed to the request of the Soviet Union to convene the sixth session of the Council of Foreign Ministers (CFM), the fifth CFM having met before the imposition of the blockade. The sixth CFM, which began on 21 May 1949, produced the last quadripartite agreement on Berlin before 1971. It was released in the form of a quadripartite communiqué on 20 June 1949.

In the communiqué the four powers agreed that the occupation authorities would continue to consult in Berlin on a "quadripartite basis" and would "continue their efforts to achieve the restoration of the economic and political unity of Germany." Future meetings were to center on the discussion of three points: (1) the mitigation of "the effects of the present administrative division of Germany and of Berlin" in the areas of "trade and development of the financial and economic relations between the western zones and the eastern zone and between Berlin and the zones"; (2) the facilitation of the "movement of persons and goods and the exchange of information between the western zones and the eastern zone and between Berlin and the zones"; and (3) consideration of "questions of common interest relating to the administration of the four sectors in Berlin with a view to normalizing as far as possible the life of the city." [10]

The communiqué empowered the respective occupation authorities to call upon "German experts and appropriate German organizations . . . for assistance" in drawing up initial documents and subsequent revisions for agreements in these areas. So far as transportation and communication between Berlin and the zones was concerned, the

---

[9] *Documents, 1944-1959,* pp. 59-60.

[10] Ibid., pp. 63-64.

13

communiqué declared that each of the occupation authorities in his own zone "will have an obligation to take the measures necessary to ensure the normal functioning and utilization of rail, water, and road transport for such movement of persons and goods and such communications by post, telephone and telegraph."

On the question of Western access to the Allied sectors of Berlin, the communiqué stated that "the New York Agreement of May 4, 1949, shall be maintained." The relevant passage of that agreement read: "All the restrictions imposed since March 1, 1948 by the Government of the Union of the Soviet Socialist Republics on communications, transportation, and trade between Berlin and the Western Zones of Germany and between the Eastern Zone and the Western Zones will be removed on May 12, 1949." [11]

Restrictions on communications, transportation, and trade between Berlin and the four zones of occupation were lifted following the blockade. But there existed no prior agreement in writing specifically stating that civilian traffic between Berlin and West Germany be free and unrestricted. There may have been an "understanding" at one time that this question would be settled directly by the military commanders in the Control Council in Berlin. But none of the three Western powers concluded an agreement with the Soviet Union on the question of civilian access by rail, road, or water to the "special Berlin area," although the United States insisted upon agreements with Great Britain to ensure access to the American enclave of Bremen within the British zone. In 1945 it was apparently believed that the right of occupation included the right of access to and from Berlin. The Western powers did not insist on concluding separate agreements governing access to Berlin following their occupation of the city because they did not wish to generate unnecessary Soviet suspicion or make it difficult—or more difficult than it was—to cooperate with the Soviet Union in Berlin.[12]

It is important to note that in 1945 the common assumption was that the occupation of Berlin would be brief, pending the formation of a unified German government. The creation of a "special Berlin area"

---

11 Ibid., pp. 59-60.
12 See Lucius D. Clay, *Decision in Germany* (Garden City, N.Y.: Doubleday & Company, 1950), especially Chapters 2 and 3; and Dennis L. Bark, *Die Berlin-Frage 1949-1955: Verhandlungsgrundlagen und Eindämmungspolitik* (Berlin: Walter de Gruyter, 1972), pp. 19-27.

14

was consistent with the division of Germany into zones of occupation.[13] It was assumed that the occupation of Germany would be temporary pending the establishment of a postwar German government. Therefore the logical location for the occupation regime, the Control Council, was in the city that was the former and presumably future German capital. Thus, the special Berlin area was created within the Soviet zone, divided into sectors to correspond to the division of Germany, and placed under quadripartite administration. It followed that the occupation of Berlin would cease at the same time that a new German government had been created in Berlin and the occupation of Germany came to an end.

For these reasons there was no quadripartite agreement on civilian access to and from Berlin, with the exception of the reference to the "normal functioning and utilization of rail, water, and road transport for such movement of persons and goods" contained in the communiqué of 20 June 1949. In the absence of any specific agreement governing access, the West considered right of access to be implicitly guaranteed with the right of occupation of the city. It was in principle established by 1970, although the Soviet and East German governments were not explicitly denied the ability to interfere with these modes of transportation at their discretion. This explains why one of the main purposes of the 1970-71 negotiations on Berlin was to gain an agreement in writing concerning unrestricted access to and from Berlin.

The issue of access, however, was not the only problem that would cause difficulties. At the sixth CFM the foreign ministers failed to reach

---

[13] Cf. Philip E. Mosely, "The Occupation of Germany: New Light on How the Zones Were Drawn," *Foreign Affairs,* vol. 28 (July 1950), pp. 580-604. There are a number of analyses of the Berlin problem and several times as many articles presenting a history of the crises that have plagued the city. Particular attention should be drawn to the following, all of which contain very useful bibliographies: Lucius D. Clay, *Decision in Germany;* W. Phillips Davison, *The Berlin Blockade* (Princeton: Princeton University, 1958); Hans Speier, *Divided Berlin: The Anatomy of Soviet Political Blackmail* (New York: Frederick Praeger, 1961); Philip Windsor, *City on Leave* (New York: Frederick Praeger, 1963); Alois Riklin, *Das Berlin-problem* (Cologne: Verlag Wissenschaft und Politik, 1964); Jürgen Fijalkowski et al., *Berlin: Hauptstadtanspruch und Westintegration* (Cologne: Westdeutscher Verlag, 1967); Dennis L. Bark, *Die Berlin-Frage 1949-1955;* Hans Herzfeld, *Berlin in der Weltpolitik 1945-1970* (Berlin: Walter de Gruyter, 1973); Diethelm Prowe, *Weltstadt in Krisen: Berlin 1949-1958* (Berlin: Walter de Gruyter, 1973). As of this writing the documents of British foreign policy relating to the occupation of Berlin and of Germany have not been released. Included in these papers are those of the Attlee Commission, and these should be especially helpful concerning the reasons for the occupation of Berlin within the Soviet zone of occupation.

agreement on the means of restoring unity to Greater Berlin. No agreements of major importance were achieved during the quadripartite discussions held in Berlin from June through September 1949. Berlin remained divided. Slowly the division assumed a more concrete character and, by 1970, the character of permanency, with the Western sectors of Berlin almost completely isolated from the Soviet sector and from their natural hinterland in East Germany.

Berlin: 1949 through 1957

Following the sixth Council of Foreign Ministers the Berlin situation underwent gradual change. The Federal Republic of Germany (formerly the Western zones of occupation) and the German Democratic Republic (formerly the Soviet zone of occupation) were officially created in September and October of 1949. According to the constitution of the German Democratic Republic, the Soviet sector of Berlin was the declared state capital "Berlin." East Berlin became the seat of the East German parliament, the Volkskammer, as well as the location of the GDR's government offices. The Soviet Union did place a limitation on East Berlin's representatives to the Volkskammer, giving them only an advisory vote.

The integration of the Soviet sector with the GDR was made more complete than that of West Berlin with the Federal Republic although West Berlin maintains a unique relationship with West Germany. Articles 23 and 144(2) of the Basic Law (*Grundgesetz*) of the Federal Republic, promulgated in 1949, foresaw the inclusion of "Greater Berlin" as the twelfth *Land* (state) of West Germany. The three Western powers however, in accordance with their observance of the 1944-45 agreements governing the "special Berlin area," suspended these two articles when they approved the Basic Law.[14] The representatives of West Berlin's government to the Bundestag and the Bundesrat were thus allowed to vote only in an advisory capacity. West Berlin residents could not vote in West German elections. West German citizens of draftable age who resided in West Berlin were not required to serve in the West German army (*Bundeswehr*). Legislation passed by the West German Bundestag did not apply automatically to Berlin. In

---

[14] The English translation "Basic Law" was formulated in 1949 to indicate that prior to the reunification of Germany the Federal Republic did not have a "Constitution" (*Verfassung*).

practice, however, such legislation has usually been adopted by the West Berlin parliament according to a special procedure approved by the Kommandatura.[15]

Even though West Berlin was not permitted to become a "constituent" part of the Federal Republic by the Western powers, it became so closely connected that it was in reality a true part of the Federal Republic. The three main political parties in West Berlin, the Social Democratic Party (SPD), the Christian Democratic Union (CDU) and the Free Democratic Party (FDP), were each constituent parts of their respective national parties whose headquarters are in Bonn. The mayor of West Berlin assumed the presidency of the Bundesrat on a revolving basis as one of the heads of the *Länder* of the Federal Republic. Since the Soviet sector had been separated from Greater Berlin by the Soviet Union and the organs of the GDR government established there, it was necessary for the West German government to establish its own federal presence in West Berlin to demonstrate the city's ties with the Federal Republic. This had to be done in a manner consistent with the city's four-power status. The visits and meetings of federal officials and the constitutional acts they performed in West Berlin served an important psychological, economic, and political purpose: they emphasized that the West Berliners, despite their geographical isolation, were not isolated from the Federal Republic in other respects. Therefore, since the founding of the Federal Republic of Germany (*Bundesrepublik*) in 1949, each meeting of the National Assembly (*Bundesversammlung*), held to elect the president of the Federal Republic, took place in Berlin. Bundestag committee meetings and party caucuses were held there several times a year. Various cultural, scientific, political, and economic organizations from the Federal Republic also met regularly in West Berlin. The degrees awarded by West Berlin's universities were accorded the same recognition as those awarded by universities in the Federal Republic. In addition federal offices representing various West German ministries and agencies were located in West Berlin. By 1970 these employed approximately 20,000 persons. Without these connections

---

[15] For the documents pertaining to the administration of Berlin under four-power occupation, the division of the city, and the relationship of the four sectors to East and West Germany, see the following: *Dokumente zur Berlin-Frage 1944-1966*, 3d ed., Forschungsinstitut der Deutschen Gesellschaft für Auswärtige Politik, e. V., vol. 18 (Munich: R. Oldenbourg, 1967) and *Berlin: Quellen und Dokumente 1945-1951*, Schriftenreihe zur Berliner Zeitgeschichte, vol. 4 (Berlin: Heinz Spitzing Verlag, 1964; published for the West Berlin Senat in 2 volumes).

with the Federal Republic it is likely the city would have been unable to survive.

Life in the Western sectors of Berlin remained tense. The city was isolated from West Germany. Traffic by road, rail, and water was plagued by continual harassment. Berliners followed with intense interest those world problems with possible consequences for the security of Berlin and the city's population. Nonetheless, West Berlin was an exciting place to live and to visit. Its citizens had strong nerves and a quick humor. They had no alternative but "to laugh in the teeth of whatever is new and scary." In West Berlin's cafes, which had attracted musicians and visitors from East and West for decades, the Berliners continued "to sing the songs and spin in the dances" of their Eastern European neighbors, whose governments were their enemies.[16]

Of course, the atmosphere could not be described as normal. The imagination and spirit of the West Berliners had made the city grow and prosper, but not at the same rate as cities in the Federal Republic and not without considerable sacrifice. The city's economy was dependent upon substantial financial support from the West German government. Its physical safety was dependent on the strength of the political commitment to its preservation by the Federal Republic, France, Great Britain, and the United States, and on the military commitment of NATO.

Normal civic responsibilities were often overshadowed by difficulties not common to other large cities such as Munich or Hamburg. In 1952 the East German government severed the telephone lines connecting West Berlin with East Berlin and the German Democratic Republic. In the same year the border between West Berlin and East Germany was sealed. Roads were blocked by barbed wire and the borders patrolled by armed guards. Pavement was torn up on most streets between the Soviet sector and West Berlin, making them impassable for motor vehicles. Where the border line ran through farms, houses and barns were divided.

In 1954 the seventh Council of Foreign Ministers, held in Berlin, did not produce an accord on any issue concerning Berlin or Germany. The Geneva summit conference that followed in the summer of 1955 also adjourned without resolving any major German issue.

---

[16] See Richard Atcheson, "Berlin for Night Life," *Travel & Leisure* (October-November 1971), pp. 38, 76-77.

Between 1955 and 1958 Berlin was without a major crisis. There continued to be occasional harassment on the autobahns and in and around the city. (Harassment within the city was possible when traveling between the Soviet sector and West Berlin or between West Berlin and the twelve small exclaves surrounding it. These exclaves are in East Germany, but belong to West Berlin.) Interzonal tolls were increased 1,000 percent in 1955 and later partially reduced. Very often traffic lights at the border crossings would be switched from green to red for many hours. Detailed inspections of luggage and, infrequently, physical examinations would be conducted; books and other belongings were arbitrarily confiscated, and automobiles themselves were impounded. Non-German citizens were forced to replace their license plates with those of the German Democratic Republic for the two-hour journey between Berlin and the Federal Republic. On a bad day, the two-hour journey could take twenty hours or more.

Harassment or the threat of it created serious difficulties. The West Berlin government had to embark on a program designed to attract young West Germans to settle in Berlin. This was necessary to balance an aging population: approximately 20 percent of the Berliners were 65 or over, compared to an average for West German cities of 12 percent. Success in the program would increase the working force and thereby the vitality of the city's population. But the uncertainties of border crossing tended to discourage young West Germans from moving to West Berlin. For many, it was preferable to live in a West German city and be free to make short trips into the countryside without experiencing prolonged border controls and luggage inspections. The only way to avoid potential harassment was to travel to and from Berlin by air, which was a comparatively expensive alternative to land transit in spite of subsidies paid by the West German government to the city's commercial carriers.

Harassment not only affected West Berlin's economy adversely by making residence less desirable than in West Germany (and tourists less plentiful), but it also tended to discourage large capital investment in the city. There were two reasons for this: the political uncertainty over the future of Berlin, and the expense involved with transporting goods to and from the city. Formal protests by the Western powers were unable to prevent interference with the interzonal traffic.

On 20 September 1955, in the Bolz-Zorin agreement, the Soviet Union granted the German Democratic Republic the control of rail, road, and water traffic between West Berlin and West Germany. All traffic, with the exception of French, British, and American military vehicles, was thereafter subject to East German control, although Soviet officers remained posted at the border checkpoints. This action was intended to demonstrate that the German Democratic Republic was a sovereign state and to force the Western Allies to recognize it as such. Moreover, by dealing with East Germany, it was hoped that the Western Allies would relieve the Soviet government of all responsibility it had assumed as a party to the quadripartite agreements of 1944, 1945, and 1949.[17]

The Bolz-Zorin agreement is instructive. The Soviet recognition of East Germany at first glance was a quid pro quo. One week earlier on 13 September, the Soviet Union had recognized the Federal Republic, and it would seem to follow that it ought to recognize East Germany as well. However, in its recognition of West Germany Moscow specifically did not recognize West Germany's claim to West Berlin, while in the second agreement it did recognize East Germany's claim to East Berlin. The wording was ambiguous enough so that it took years before the Soviet Union was forced to agree that it was still ultimately responsible for access to West Berlin even though East German soldiers manned the border check points.

Berlin: 1958 through 1961

In November 1958 the Berlin situation again became agitated. Premier Nikita Khrushchev delivered an ultimatum to the three Western powers in which he declared the quadripartite agreement of 12 September 1944 and the related supplementary agreements to be "null and void." He proposed that discussions begin within six months in order to transform West Berlin into a free city. In the event the Western powers declined Premier Khrushchev's offer, the note declared, the Soviet government would begin negotiations with East Germany for the purpose of transferring to the German Democratic Republic "the functions temporarily

---

[17] See the letter from the foreign minister of the German Democratic Republic, Lothar Bolz, to the Soviet deputy foreign minister, V. A. Zorin, on the transfer of certain control functions from Russian to East German authorities, 20 September 1955, in *Documents, 1944-1959*, pp. 156-158ff. Also see the series of notes exchanged between the United States and the Soviet Union in the *U.S. Department of State Bulletin*, 10 October 1955, pp. 559-560; 17 October 1955, p. 616; 7 November 1955, pp. 734-735.

performed" by the Soviet Union according to quadripartite agreements on Berlin and according to the Bolz-Zorin agreement of 20 September 1955.[18]

This threat to the security of West Berlin touched off a continuing crisis that lasted until after the construction of the Berlin Wall in August 1961. During the early period intensive negotiations were conducted with the Soviet Union in Geneva. Although no agreement was concluded, the ultimatum was left dangling while the world's attention focused on Premier Khrushchev's visit to the United States in 1959, the abortive Paris summit conference in 1960, and the Vienna meeting between President Kennedy and Premier Khrushchev in June 1961.

During the prolonged security crisis, the flow of refugees from East Germany to West Berlin and West Germany continued to increase. The loss of manpower was a serious drain on the economies of East Germany and East Berlin. And to the extent that the Soviet commandant was responsible for the well-being of his sector according to the agreements of 1944-45 and 1949, the loss of manpower could be considered his legitimate concern, even though he had violated those agreements on numerous occasions in the past. Following the Vienna meeting in June 1961, the flow of refugees rose sharply despite Walter Ulbricht's assurances on 15 June 1961 that "no one has the intention of building a wall." At the beginning of August 1961, East German citizens were entering West Berlin at the rate of several thousand a day.

In the early morning of 13 August 1961, East German soldiers sealed the border with barbed wire and, in the days following, the Wall was completed. Although building the Wall violated the spirit of earlier agreements concerning movement across zones, it violated no explicit four-power agreement. Notwithstanding the Soviet Union's arbitrary termination of the quadripartite administration of Greater Berlin in 1948, the four-power agreements themselves remained valid, and the commandants retained supreme authority in their respective sectors. The Soviet commandant's authority in his sector was respected by the Western powers. Theoretically this authority extended to the construction of buildings, roads, or walls. Had the Wall on the border of the Soviet sector been removed by the Western powers, it could have been rebuilt several hundred yards inside the Soviet sector. Had the

---

[18] *Documents, 1944-1959*, pp. 317-331.

Western powers then chosen to raze the Wall, the legal onus for precipitating a crisis would have rested with them.

Berlin: 1962 through 1968

The presence of the Wall served as a new focus for West Berlin's attention. Between 1961 and 1963 attention centered on assisting East Germans to escape the GDR and East Berlin. The longer the Wall stood, the more difficult escape to West Berlin became (and by 1970, at least sixty-four refugees attempting to escape to West Berlin had been killed by East German border guards). Frustration at West Berlin's inability to alter the situation grew. Demonstrations against the policies of the Soviet and East German governments had no effect. By 1966 student protest in West Berlin was no longer directed primarily toward the dictatorship that built the Wall; it was directed instead toward the foreign policies of the free and democratic governments of the West which still preserved the city's freedom but which had been unable to remove the Wall.

In the official terminology of the Soviet and East German governments, West Berlin had become an "independent political entity" by 1964 when this phrase was used in the treaty of friendship and mutual assistance concluded between the GDR and the Soviet Union. West Berlin had never been considered by either the Soviet Union or East Germany to belong to the Federal Republic or to be under its administration. Legally this position was correct, because Articles 23 and 144(2) of the West German Basic Law remained suspended by the Western powers. But the Western powers in Berlin had permitted the establishment of ties demonstrating West Berlin's economic, social, cultural, and political unity with the Federal Republic.

In the 1960s, as in the previous decade, on almost every occasion that the "demonstrative federal presence" was exercised in West Berlin, whether by a visit from the chancellor or by Bundestag committee meetings, traffic on the autobahns was harassed. Displeasure was also conveyed by other means. For example, Soviet and East German military aircraft welcomed the 1965 meeting of the Bundestag in West Berlin by breaking thousands of windows with sonic booms.

Between 1964 and 1966 the East German government concluded temporary "pass agreements" with the Federal Republic permitting West Berliners to visit their relatives in the Soviet sector. Unfortunately these

22

agreements were not renewed after 1966. Only on the occasion of the serious illness or death of a relative was a small number of West Germans allowed to cross the Wall.

In 1968 East Germany provoked another crisis by attempting to assert its sovereignty over the access routes through the imposition of transit visas and attendant fees on West Germans and West Berliners using road and rail connections across East Germany. After considerable discussion among the Allies, and between the Allies and West Germany, West German recommendations were followed; the visas and fees were agreed to, and the West German government increased its subsidy to West Berlin. The episode served to underscore the difficulties inherent in the Western position. While the United States, Britain, and France were committed to the defense of West Berlin, they could only protect her interests as the West German government defined them. If West Germany wanted to accede to a Soviet or East German assertion so as to minimize momentary disadvantages, the three powers could not prevent it.[19]

By the late 1960s West Berlin's economy was strong and growing. Democratic government in the city had proved viable. President Nixon made it clear during his visit to West Berlin on 27 February 1969 that "no unilateral move, no illegal act, no form of pressure from any source will shake the resolve of the Western Powers to defend their rightful status as protectors of the people of free Berlin." As the President emphasized, "the question before the world," was not whether the West would "rise to the challenge of defending Berlin" but whether the situation in Berlin would be viewed by both sides "as an invocation to action." [20]

The Changing Diplomatic Climate: Early 1969

President Nixon's visit to Berlin in February 1969 increased discussion of the possibility for new negotiations to ease the Berlin situation. The United States took the first step in its effort to open negotiations almost two weeks before Richard Nixon's inauguration. In early January Nixon announced that he planned to visit Europe that year to discuss

---

[19] Eleanor Lansing Dulles, *One Germany or Two: The Struggle at the Heart of Europe* (Stanford: Hoover Institution, 1970), pp. 147-148.

[20] President Richard M. Nixon in an address to the workers of the Siemens plant in West Berlin, 27 February 1969.

23

NATO and other problems of European security. On 6 February 1969 he said that his visit to Europe that month would include stops at Bonn, Berlin, Brussels, London, Paris and Rome. In the meantime on 11 January the Soviet ambassador to the Federal Republic of Germany had proposed to Foreign Minister Brandt that talks between the Soviet Union and West Germany—which had been discontinued in July 1968, prior to the Czechoslovakian invasion—be resumed. The ambassador suggested that the subjects of the talks should include a conference on European security and the reduction of troops in Europe. On the day of Nixon's inauguration, 20 January 1969, the Soviet Union proposed the renewal of discussions with the United States on the limitation of strategic arms. These proposals, less than six months after the invasion of Czechoslovakia, were important. They were the preliminary steps in the effort to transform confrontation into cooperation.

During his visit to Europe that February, President Nixon emphasized that American interest in Europe had never been greater and that a stable Europe had never been more necessary for world peace. The fact that this was the President's first trip outside the United States and the fact that it was made only five weeks after his inauguration drew special attention to this point. In his discussion with European leaders he stressed the necessity for negotiations with the Soviet Union and the countries of Eastern Europe, while emphasizing the importance of a unified Western position. His discussions with European leaders centered on joint concerns: arms control, the Middle East, the future of NATO, bilateral negotiations between the states of Eastern and Western Europe, and Berlin.[21]

The President's visit to Berlin on 27 February was also notable because it occurred at a time when the German Democratic Republic was harassing traffic between West Berlin and West Germany in retaliation for the West German government's decision to hold the presidential election meeting of the Bundesversammlung in the city on 5 March. (Since 1954 this National Assembly had been held every fifth year in Berlin.) Although the East German government had welcomed the election at that time, East Germany and the Soviet Union now said the meeting violated Berlin's quadripartite status. Before the President's visit, the Soviet Union had delivered several protests to the three Western powers and to the West German government. President Nixon's

---

21 *Die Welt,* 24, 25 and 27 February, and 6 March 1969.

arrival in the city a week before the election showed the West's commitment to the defense of Berlin—specifically to the defense of the "three essentials" for the freedom of West Berlin first defined by President Kennedy in 1961: (1) safeguarding free access to and from Berlin, (2) stationing Western garrisons in Berlin, and (3) maintaining the city's cultural, political, and economic viability.[22]

The West German government supported Nixon's Berlin announcement that the United States welcomed negotiations with the Soviet Union on ways to diminish tension in the city. The Federal Republic's Chancellor Kurt Georg Kiesinger, a member of the Christian Democratic party, announced during the President's visit to Bonn that the Federal Republic would undertake its own initiatives to improve relations with Eastern Europe.[23]

Not all the momentum for improved East-West relations was supplied by the determined efforts of Western leaders. At the beginning of March 1969 the first reports of border incidents between Chinese and Soviet troops on the Ussuri River were published in Europe. The Soviet ambassador to West Germany paid a special and unprecedented visit to Chancellor Kiesinger to explain the dispute between the Chinese and the Soviet governments. The Soviet government did not want the United States and West Germany to try to exploit the rift for their own purposes. It may be noted that when the Bundesversammlung was held without incident, the Chinese concluded that the absence of a crisis was attributable to collusion between the Soviet Union and the United States.[24]

The Sino-Soviet dispute also affected the position of the Warsaw Pact states on East-West relations. At the Warsaw Pact conference in mid-March 1969, Rumania refused to accede to the Soviet demand that the Warsaw Treaty Organization (WTO) issue a communiqué condemning China. Rumania argued that the Warsaw Pact was responsible for Europe but not for Asian questions. The WTO did, however, adopt a unified position on Western Europe. For the first time since July 1966, the WTO proposed a conference on European security. In its final communiqué the WTO endorsed peaceful coexistence and the replacement of confrontation with cooperation between Eastern and Western Europe. It also demanded the recognition of all European

---

[22] Address by President John F. Kennedy, 26 July 1961.
[23] *Die Welt,* 27 February 1969.
[24] Ibid., 6 and 10 March 1969.

borders, including the one dividing Germany and the Oder-Neisse line, diplomatic recognition of the German Democratic Republic, renunciation of the use of force by West Germany, and the repudiation of the Hallstein doctrine.[25]

Sino-Soviet border incidents continued through March and April. Rumors began to appear in the West German press of a possible preventive nuclear strike by the Soviet Union against China. The seriousness of the dispute suggested that the Soviet Union might be trying to create a stable relationship in Europe while increasing troop strength along the Chinese border. West German Chancellor Kiesinger believed that the Sino-Soviet dispute was responsible for improvement in the Soviet attitude toward relations with the Federal Republic. While Soviet representatives in Western European capitals continued to explain their government's position on the Chinese dispute, the United States announced that it would not seek to exploit the Sino-Soviet rift, and that it would seek to improve relations with China.[26]

The movement for diplomatic change gathered additional momentum in April and May. Foreign Minister Brandt stressed the importance of Western European unity as a prerequisite for negotiations with the East, and criticized a possible "senseless race" of Western European countries for contacts with Eastern Europe. Secretary of State Rogers announced on 9 April that the United States planned to discuss limitations of strategic weapons with the Soviet Union. He also announced that ways to improve traffic to and from Berlin would be discussed with Foreign Minister Brandt during his visit to the United States in the middle of April for the twentieth anniversary meeting of NATO.[27]

Following President Nixon's address to the April NATO meeting —in which he said that the old concept of East against West must be replaced with cooperation between East and West—Brandt urged that NATO should consider discussing the possibility of a conference on European security with the Warsaw Pact states. He pointed out that the NATO ministers had proposed discussion of issues of European

---

[25] Ibid., 15, 17, 18 and 20 March 1969. By the Hallstein doctrine West Germany asserted that it represented all German people in both parts of Germany and discontinued or refused to grant diplomatic recognition to any state which recognized East Germany. Among the glaring irregularities in the application of this doctrine may be noted the fact that West Germany had recognized the U.S.S.R. since 1955.

[26] Ibid., 3, 4 and 5 April 1969.

[27] Ibid., 10 April 1969.

security with the WTO at its Reykjavik meeting in June 1968. But he also said that while the Soviet Union was seeking to dispel unpleasant memories of the Czechoslovakian invasion by conciliatory gestures toward Western Europe, "the West may not pursue détente on a selective basis, which would permit the Soviet Union to decide where to pursue détente and where to continue the cold war." In a communiqué released at the end of the conference the NATO ministers advocated increased contact with Eastern Europe.[28]

At the end of April Brandt announced that the most important goal of West Germany's foreign policy was to improve relations with the Soviet government. At the beginning of May, West Germany's *Bundesforschungsminister* (federal research minister), Gerhard Stoltenberg, visited the Soviet Union as the first West German official to travel in Eastern Europe since the invasion of Czechoslovakia. Later that month the West German government, in response to a proposal by Poland, announced that it would be prepared to discuss a mutual renunciation of force agreement with the Polish government, and also suggested that it would consider discussing Poland's border with East Germany—the Oder-Neisse line.

The third International Meeting of Communist and Workers' Parties was held in Moscow from 5 June to 17 June 1969. At the request of the Preparatory Committee, the meeting had been postponed several times, first because of the Czechoslovakian crisis and later because of the Sino-Soviet dispute. Of the fourteen ruling parties only nine were represented. China, North Korea, North Vietnam, Albania, and Yugoslavia did not attend. The meeting centered on discussion of the Czechoslovakian invasion and China. Nicolae Ceauşescu, the party leader in Rumania, criticized the condemnation of China, emphasizing that the interference in the internal affairs of one Socialist country by another violated the principle of sovereignty. In the final communiqué, all members of the Warsaw Pact declared their support for the establishment of lasting security in Europe. The communiqué called for the dissolution of NATO and the WTO and endorsed the proposals of the prior WTO conference. Like the Budapest communiqué, the Moscow communiqué demanded: (1) the inviolability of all European borders, including the Oder-Neisse line and the border dividing Germany, (2) diplomatic recognition of the German Democratic Republic, (3) West

---

[28] Ibid., 11 and 14 April 1969.

27

German renunciation of nuclear weapons, and (4) West German renunciation of the Hallstein doctrine. In addition to those proposals in the Budapest communiqué, the Moscow communiqué demanded (5) the recognition of West Berlin as a "separate political entity," and (6) West German recognition that the Munich Pact was invalid from the outset.[29]

Nevertheless, the West continued to send "feelers" east. The United States government announced at the end of June that President Nixon would visit Rumania in late July or early August to discuss the expansion of East-West trade. Shortly thereafter the West German government announced it wished to resume its discussions with the Soviet Union on an agreement for the mutual renunciation of force. These were talks the Soviet Union had also previously indicated its desire to resume. And while the situation in the Middle East was tense, the United States was exploring ways to decrease tension between Israel and the Arab states, ways generally based on Soviet assistance. Egypt's diplomatic recognition of East Germany also contributed to the continuing change in relations. Egypt, which was significantly dependent on the Soviet Union for its defense, was the sixth "non-aligned" state to accord diplomatic recognition to the German Democratic Republic at the beginning of July. It was not so much Egypt's recognition of East Germany that was significant as West Germany's decision to renounce the Hallstein doctrine in June, since Egypt's action foreshadowed growing pressure on the West German government to recognize the East German government.

Proposals for Negotiations Are Accepted

This growing pressure was influenced by Soviet Foreign Minister Gromyko's speech to the Supreme Soviet on 10 July. Foreign Minister Gromyko endorsed talks with the United States on strategic arms limitations as well as talks with the Federal Republic on the mutual renunciation of force. He expressed the Soviet government's desire to improve relations with West Germany so long as the improvement was not made at the expense of East Germany. On the question of Berlin, the foreign minister announced that in the interest of détente the Soviet

---

[29] Richard F. Staar, ed., *1970 Yearbook on International Communist Affairs* (Stanford: Hoover Institution, 1971), pp. 789-822.

28

government was prepared to discuss the Berlin question with the Western powers.[30]

The West responded to Gromyko's invitation for discussions on Berlin in early August, shortly after President Nixon's visit to Rumania. The Western powers proposed discussion of traffic to and from Berlin and discussion of methods to prevent future crises in the city. *Die Welt* reported on 8 August that the Western Allies also approved of discussions between the German Democratic Republic and the Federal Republic on traffic and postal questions concerning both parts of Germany, providing the talks could be kept within the sphere of four-power responsibility for Germany and Greater Berlin. The paper continued that the West had expressed this view to the Soviet Union hoping that the Soviet Union would encourage East Germany to participate.

While the West was formulating its response on Berlin, Helmut Allardt, the Federal Republic's ambassador to the Soviet Union, met with Premier Kosygin to discuss the possibility of resuming the discussions on the agreement for mutual renunciation of force. At this time Premier Kosygin announced to the leaders of West Germany's Free Democratic Party, who were visiting Moscow, that the Soviet Union desired better economic, technical, and cultural relations with the Federal Republic.

Chancellor Kiesinger traveled to Washington in August to discuss with President Nixon the continuing efforts to initiate a process of détente. A few days earlier Foreign Minister Brandt had announced that the Federal Republic desired discussions with the Soviet Union, Poland and Czechoslovakia on questions of European security. Kiesinger emphasized two points that were and would continue to be of special importance for the West German government. West Germany's first concern was that the United States should not reduce its troop strength in Europe before negotiations with the Soviet Union. The government's second concern was that negotiations with the Soviet Union should not take place until NATO formed a unified approach to the issues under consideration. During the meeting both men expressed hopes that negotiations on Berlin would be forthcoming. Following the meeting, West Berlin's Mayor Klaus Schütz characterized negotiations on Berlin as a test case for productive discussion of other problems of European security.[31]

---

[30] *Die Welt,* 11 July 1969.
[31] Ibid., 2, 9 and 18 August 1969.

Prospects for negotiations ebbed slightly in September. The Soviet government had not yet proposed a date to the United States for the beginning of talks on strategic arms limitations. This together with Premier Kosygin's visit with Chou En-lai, the first meeting of Chinese and Soviet leaders since 1965, led to questions about the sincerity of the Soviet attitude toward discussions of European problems. Foreign Minister Gromyko's address to the United Nations on 19 September in which he warned that peace was threatened by a "dangerous development of militarism and revanchism" in West Germany did not inspire confidence. Nor did the announcement on 6 October that Chinese and Soviet representatives would begin discussions on a solution to the border disputes suggest that the Soviet Union would have any desire to ease the Berlin problem.[32]

In the meantime, federal elections were held in West Germany in September. The Christian Democrat/Christian Socialist bloc (CDU/CSU) won a plurality but not a majority of the seats in the Bundestag. The Social Democratic party (SPD) and the Free Democratic party (FDP) each won fewer seats than the CDU/CSU, but they formed a coalition giving them a slim twelve-seat majority.

Since December 1966, the SPD had been a part of a coalition government dominated by the CDU/CSU bloc. While this coalition had taken major steps to improve West Germany's relations with Eastern Europe and the Soviet Union, the CDU/CSU was strongly opposed to recognition of the German Democratic Republic, of the Oder-Neisse line, and of the inviolability of European borders.

Before assuming the position of chancellor as the leader of the SPD, Willy Brandt had served as the foreign minister in the Kiesinger government, and prior to that he had been the mayor of West Berlin. As chancellor he was in a position to push his programs more strongly than he could as foreign minister. He introduced his approach in his first address to the Bundestag on 28 October.

Although this address was primarily devoted to domestic issues, it did indicate clearly that the Federal Republic would continue to seek cooperation with all Eastern European states, including East Germany and the Soviet Union. This search, Brandt emphasized, would proceed from a basis of Western unity. He renewed the Federal Republic's offer to the Council of Ministers of the German Democratic Republic to

---

[32] Ibid., 20 September and 7 October 1969.

discuss ways to improve relations between the two Germanys. (This offer was first presented by the SPD-CDU/CSU coalition in April 1967.) He also proposed the conclusion of an agreement with East Germany on the mutual renunciation of force. But here he made it clear that the Federal Republic could not entertain discussions centered on the recognition of the German Democratic Republic. He concluded by endorsing the efforts of France, Great Britain, and the United States to discuss with the Soviet Union questions of traffic within Greater Berlin and from Berlin to West Germany.[33]

The initiatives and proposals of the first ten months of 1969 began to bear fruit in November and December. The United States and the Soviet Union announced that the Strategic Arms Limitation Talks (SALT) would open 17 November in Helsinki. The foreign ministers of the Warsaw Pact states, meeting in Prague, proposed that a conference on European security be scheduled for the middle of 1970. West German Foreign Minister Walter Scheel announced on 11 November that the Federal Republic would shortly begin negotiations with the Soviet Union on an agreement for mutual renunciation of force. On 16 November the Federal Republic delivered its formal proposal to the Soviet government and announced its wish that negotiations on Berlin coincide with its talks with the Soviet Union. On 22 November West Germany signed the nuclear nonproliferation treaty, and on 3 December State Department spokesman Carl Bartch declared that the United States supported the efforts of the West German government to reduce tensions in Europe.[34]

At the beginning of December the NATO foreign ministers, meeting in Brussels, agreed to make consideration of Western participation in a future conference on European security dependent on the Soviet Union's attitudes toward Berlin, toward West Germany's efforts to achieve a modus vivendi with East Germany, and toward the Western proposal to reduce troops in Eastern and Western Europe. Meanwhile the leaders of the Warsaw Pact states met in Moscow, where they endorsed all efforts to improve relations with West Germany, while demanding recognition of the Oder-Neisse line and the German Democratic Republic.

Representatives of the Federal Republic of Germany met with representatives of the Soviet Union for the first official meeting to

---

[33] Ibid., 29 October 1969.
[34] Ibid., 1 November and 4 December 1969.

discuss the mutual renunciation of force on 7 December in Moscow. On 10 December Foreign Minister Scheel announced that the Federal Republic wished to begin negotiations with Czechoslovakia. On the next day representatives of the East and West German governments met to discuss traffic and postal questions. On 16 December, France, Great Britain and the United States proposed to the Soviet Union that discussions be held on the Berlin question and implied that improvements in Berlin would increase the probability of convening a conference on European security.[35]

Presumably in response to Chancellor Brandt's offer to begin negotiations with East Germany, the East German government submitted a nine-point draft treaty to Gustav Heinemann, president of the Federal Republic, on 17 December. In the accompanying letter, Walter Ulbricht, chairman of the Council of State of the German Democratic Republic and first secretary of the SED, proposed the establishment of diplomatic relations between the German states. Ulbricht wrote that he had empowered the chairman of the Council of Ministers, Willi Stoph, to conduct the negotiations for the GDR and proposed that they begin in January. The draft treaty contained provisions for West Germany's recognition of the intra-German border and of the Oder-Neisse line, for an agreement on the mutual renunciation of force, for the establishment of embassies in Bonn and East Berlin, for membership in the United Nations as independent sovereign states, and for the obligation "to respect the status of West Berlin as an independent political entity and in view of this status to establish their relations with West Berlin." President Heinemann's reply of 20 December indicated that the letter and the draft treaty had been delivered to the federal government which would, in turn, make an appropriate response.[36]

Summary

In the years following 1945, Berlin was a pawn in the cold war. Because quadripartite administration of the city did not work, the city's status, which should have been clear in 1945, remained disputed. Its isolated position ensured that there would not be an acceptance of the division of the city which might have occurred had the geographical

---

[35] Ibid., 17 and 19 December 1969.

[36] The text of the draft treaty is reprinted in *Der Tagesspiegel*, 23 December 1969.

division of Berlin coincided with the geographical division of Germany.[37] This position was a source of recurrent tension and occasional confrontations. Particularly severe confrontations occurred in the years 1948-49, 1958-59, and 1961. For a variety of reasons, none of them produced fruitful results.

The year 1969 marked a change in attitudes in both East and West. On the one hand, West Germany's Ostpolitik and President Nixon's desire for détente produced a new willingness on the part of the West to consider compromises that would ease the Berlin situation. On the other hand, the Soviet Union found itself with a major schism in the Communist bloc. While it was not seriously concerned with the military situation in Europe, it did not wish to give China an opportunity to make significant political gains in Eastern or Western Europe as a result of Soviet confrontation with the West. It also had the longstanding wish to legitimize the World War II division in Europe. The process of détente, as a consequence, appeared to hold advantages for both sides.

In one sense the Berlin situation was a poor test of détente. The issues were so complex, and so many parties were interested in them, that solutions could not be a simple matter of each side giving a little. Nevertheless, the Berlin negotiations were a test in the sense that both sides had serious interests in the fate of Berlin; and a mutually acceptable agreement could presage serious negotiations in other areas.

---

[37] Cf. Mahncke, "Verantwortung für Berlin," p. 118.

2

Clarification of the Issues

As President Nixon has emphasized, it was apparent in 1969 that past efforts to achieve détente in Europe had failed because nations had not dealt with the central questions of the division of Germany and Berlin, or because the attempts to deal with them created further stalemate and confrontation.[1] It was imperative that East and West make their positions as clear as possible before the start of negotiations on Berlin.

But Berlin was so closely related to the problem of European security that it was not clear whether a decision to begin new quadripartite negotiations on Berlin could be made independent of efforts to begin negotiations on other subjects. It was not at all certain in 1969 how many, if any, of the differences that had arisen among the four powers over Berlin could be resolved in a mutually satisfactory manner. Not only did the four powers have to be satisfied, but also any agreement they made would have to consider the interests of the East and West German governments and of West Berlin as well. What was certain was that Berlin was so entwined in the foreign policy of so many governments that the success of other negotiations, even those not directly related to Berlin, would influence and be influenced by the quadripartite negotiations on Berlin.

Points at Issue

The four powers had not formally agreed to convene quadripartite discussions in January 1970. The Soviet Union had not yet delivered

---

[1] Richard M. Nixon, "United States Foreign Policy for the 1970s: The Emerging Structure of Peace," report to the Congress 9 February 1972, p. 47.

an official response to the Western *aide-mémoire* on Berlin of 16 December. There was, nevertheless, a great deal of attention being devoted to the details of the Berlin question and how they related to possible negotiations to be conducted by the Federal Republic with the Soviet Union, Poland, and the German Democratic Republic.

On 10 January 1970, the East German Ministry for Foreign Affairs addressed a note to the West German government. The note declared that the caucus and committee meetings of the West German Bundestag scheduled for Berlin at the end of January were contrary to détente, contrary to the interests of the West Berliners, and in violation of the sovereign rights of the German Democratic Republic. It emphasized that "West Berlin," according to international treaties, was "an independent entity in the middle of the German Democratic Republic." The East German note recognized that the German Democratic Republic endorsed the establishment of détente, and it concluded that "the independent political entity of West Berlin is an important element in the existing territorial status quo in Europe . . . the observance of this status [was declared to be] the indispensable precondition for the guarantee of European security." [2]

This kind of protest, made neither for the first nor for the last time on 10 January, was an excellent tactic of political warfare. In ascribing a status to West Berlin that it did not have, the German Democratic Republic demanded either acceptance or denial of the ascription by the Western powers. Should a denial be forthcoming, as it was in this case, East Germany hoped to enjoy the advantage of chastising the West for ostensibly pursuing policies contrary to détente and European security. In addition, East Germany was in a position to take reprisals should West Germany violate the presumed status of West Berlin as an "independent political entity," with the expectation that reprisal would show the West the necessity for compromise with the East. Thus the Foreign Ministry of the German Democratic Republic warned on 10 January that if "illegal meetings" in West Berlin were not halted, the German Democratic Republic would take "necessary measures in protection of her sovereign rights and interests."

Despite East German protests, the West German caucus and committee meetings were held and Chancellor Brandt visited the city during the meetings. In response, the German Democratic Republic began

---

[2] Allgemeiner Deutscher Nachrichtendienst, 10 and 11 January 1970. ADN is the official East German wire service.

traffic interference on 21 January and continued it until 27 January. According to the German Democratic Republic, the chancellor's visit constituted a violation of the special status of West Berlin and was commensurate with the "spirit of the cold war" allegedly practiced by his predecessors.[3] Predictably, in its turn, the West Berlin *Senat* (senate) protested the interference with a declaration that pointed out that "Berlin is and remains for the world public the test case for the [establishment of] détente." [4]

This exchange provides an opportunity to review several of the issues requiring resolution. The GDR's first point was the contention that West Berlin was an independent political entity in the middle of East Germany. Therefore, any political activity in that city not approved by the East Germans was illegal. The second point followed from the first. Since West Berlin was in the middle of East Germany, visits to that city by West German officials violated the sovereignty of the German Democratic Republic. The third was the conclusion that there was a need for settlement of the "West Berlin problem" since it was so important to European security.

The West German refutation of the East German assertion began by denying any possibility that West Berlin was an independent political entity. On the basis of the quadripartite agreements it was neither independent nor a part of the German Democratic Republic. Moreover, the treaties referred to by the East Germans were not quadripartite agreements but treaties concluded between East Germany and other members of the Warsaw Treaty Organization.[5] In denying Berlin's political independence the quadripartite agreement specifically gave each of the four powers the right to determine the political activities to be conducted in its own sector of the city. This, of course, led to the Western refutation of the East German second point—the alleged violation of East German sovereignty. The Western powers did not accord the German Democratic Republic diplomatic recognition as a sovereign state. Therefore the German Democratic Republic could not

---

[3] *Pravda,* 25 January 1970. See also *Neues Deutschland,* 22, 24, 25 and 26 January 1970.

[4] *Der Tagesspiegel,* 28 January 1970.

[5] Of the treaties East Germany had with WTO members, the Treaty on Friendship, Mutual Assistance and Cooperation concluded with the Soviet Union on 12 June 1964 was the most specific on the rights of the German Democratic Republic in Berlin.

have any sovereign rights in West Berlin, which was not a part of the GDR. Moreover, the Soviet Union, not East Germany, was ultimately responsible for unimpeded access to and from Berlin. The Western powers were willing to agree with East Germany that West Berlin was an important element in Europe. They did not agree that there was need for the settlement of a "West Berlin problem." Rather, the need was for settlement of problems arising from differing interpretations of the quadripartite agreements of 1944-45 and 1949 on Greater Berlin.

Chancellor Brandt covered many of these points in his *Bericht zur Lage der Nation* (report on the state of the nation) delivered to the West German Bundestag on 14 January 1970. In this address he set forth the framework within which he viewed the negotiations and outlined the principles he would use to guide negotiations with the German Democratic Republic.

The chancellor believed West Germany to have a definite responsibility to aid in reducing tensions in Europe. To this end his government was engaged in discussions with the Soviet Union and was preparing a proposal for discussions with East Germany. His government was also preparing for negotiations with Poland, Czechoslovakia, and Hungary on the reduction of European tensions. He stressed that West Germany could not conduct discussions with East Germany as though it were a foreign country. The Federal Republic wished to begin discussions with the German Democratic Republic on a basis of "equality and nondiscrimination."

The six principles Chancellor Brandt outlined to guide future negotiations with the German Democratic Republic reflected the three Western powers' position in their negotiations with the Soviet Union on Berlin. Both states should respect (1) the obligation to maintain the unity of the German nation, (2) the generally recognized principles of international law (exclusion of discrimination, respect for territorial integrity, the obligation to solve all disputes peacefully, and respect for common borders), (3) the obligation not to alter the social structure in the territory of the other party, (4) the efforts of both governments to establish neighborly cooperation, (5) the existing rights and responsibilities of the four powers for Germany as a whole and for Berlin, and (6) the efforts of the four powers to reach agreements to improve the Berlin situation.[6]

---

[6] Following his address, Chancellor Brandt sent a letter to Chairman Stoph proposing "negotiations on the exchange of declarations on the renunciation of force."

In the addenda to his address, which the chancellor had submitted to the Bundestag on 11 January, he drew attention to three points the Federal Republic and the Western powers considered essential in their position on Berlin: (1) unrestricted access to and from Berlin, with a cessation of harassment on the autobahns connecting West Berlin with West Germany (*Zugang*); (2) undisputed recognition by the Soviet Union and the German Democratic Republic of West Berlin's economic, cultural and political ties with West Germany, along with the acknowledgment that federal presence in Berlin was implicit in those ties, thereby denying that West Berlin was an independent political entity (*Zuordnung*); and (3) entry for West Berliners to East Berlin and to East Germany on the same basis accorded West German citizens, as well as improvements in communications among West Berlin, the German Democratic Republic and the Soviet sector of Berlin (*Zutritt*).[7]

Five days after Chancellor Brandt's speech, Walter Ulbricht considered East and West German relations in a press conference in East Berlin. It was the first press conference to which Western journalists had been invited in more than eight years. Secretary Ulbricht endorsed détente in Europe, but his position was (predictably) quite different from Chancellor Brandt's. He demanded the diplomatic recognition of East Germany and announced that his government still expected an official response to the draft treaty he had submitted in December, which proposed the establishment of diplomatic relations between the two German governments. Ulbricht did not reject the possibility of discussions between the GDR and the Federal Republic on an agreement for mutual renunciation of force, but he declared that these could not begin before the conclusion of the negotiations between the Soviet Union and West Germany.

Secretary Ulbricht was particularly explicit in defining the East German position on the status of Berlin and the asserted existence of a "West Berlin problem" in connection with future quadripartite negotiations. In support of the German Democratic Republic's claim that it was a sovereign state with its own sovereign capital city, Ulbricht declared that "the capital city of the German Democratic Republic, Berlin . . . is not subject to four-power control." During the four-power negotiations the Wall would not be "an object of discussion. West

---

[7] See *Materialien zum Bericht zur Lage der Nation.* Deutscher Bundestag, 6. Wahlperiode, Drucksache VI/223, 11 January 1970.

Berlin is another question. But I would not like to interfere in that occupation regime." [8]

East Germany's interference with access to West Berlin and Walter Ulbricht's assertions concerning West Berlin were a serious matter. To emphasize how seriously the Western powers took the East German actions, the American ambassador to Germany delivered one of the strongest protests in years to Pyotr Abrasimov, the Soviet ambassador to the German Democratic Republic.[9] Ambassador Rush stated that West Berlin did not lie "on," "within," or "in" the middle of the East German territory, and that no part of Berlin was a part of the German Democratic Republic. At a press conference several days later Rush declared that committee meetings of the Bundestag had taken place for many years with the approval of the Western powers, and he emphasized that interference with traffic to and from Berlin constituted a violation of the four-power status of Berlin and of existing quadripartite agreements. The ambassador's statement made the Western position very clear. A representative of the Soviet embassy in East Germany dismissed the protest as untenable, asserting that there was a "four-power responsibility for West Berlin" and that West Berlin was a political entity "independent" of the Federal Republic.[10] American officials in West Berlin noted, however, that no official Soviet response had been received and that the Soviet representative did not identify himself.

Following this exchange, on 10 February the Soviet government responded to the 16 December Western note with the proposal that quadripartite negotiations on Berlin be started as soon as possible. According to reports in West German newspapers, the Soviet Union sought to restrict negotiations to discussion of West Berlin, based on an asserted quadripartite status for the Western sectors. The 16 December note had suggested that the negotiations be held alternately in East and West Berlin, since this would demonstrate quadripartite responsibility for the entire city. But the Soviet government did not refer to this proposal and suggested instead that the discussions be held solely

---

[8] *Neues Deutschland,* 20 January 1970.

[9] Ambassador Abrasimov is a member of the Central Committee of the Communist party of the Soviet Union. He was replaced as ambassador to West Germany following the conclusion of the Berlin agreement, and was himself appointed Soviet ambassador to France.

[10] *Frankfurter Allgemeine Zeitung,* 2 February 1970; *Die Welt,* 5 and 6 February 1970; *Neues Deutschland,* 2 February 1970.

in West Berlin, using the former Allied Control Council building located in the American sector. Nor did the Soviet note refer to the three proposed points for discussion raised in the Western note: (1) elimination of restrictions on contact with West Berlin (primarily of an economic nature) imposed by the Soviet Union; (2) improvement of traffic and telephone connections, and postal and trade services between the parts of Berlin; and (3) improvement in traffic of persons and goods between Berlin and West Germany.[11]

The official Western response, after consultation with the West German government, was contained in *aides-mémoire* delivered simultaneously on 27 February. France, Great Britain and the United States agreed to meet with the Soviet Union in the former Allied Control Council building in West Berlin. They proposed that the negotiations deal with improvements in and around Berlin and on the access ways. State Department spokesman Carl Bartch, in a statement issued the same day, emphasized that the *aides-mémoire* stated clearly that the Western powers would not discuss West Berlin exclusively, and the negotiations would be held "in the framework of the four-power responsibilities for all of Berlin." [12]

First Intra-German Discussion: Erfurt

In a letter to Chairman Stoph on 22 January 1970 Chancellor Brandt officially proposed intra-German discussions. This proposal followed the guidelines set forth in the *Bericht zur Lage der Nation*. Stoph responded on 11 February. The chairman invited Chancellor Brandt to meet with him in "the capital of the GDR, Berlin," adding that "negotiations on taking up relations of equal status and on renunciation of force can lead to positive results only on the basis of mutual recognition under international law." Chairman Stoph's proposal caused alarm in West Berlin and West Germany. In Bonn, Press Secretary Conrad Ahlers expressed concern that Stoph would describe Berlin as the capital of the German Democratic Republic in spite of its quadripartite status. But, he added, "that the GDR officials sit there is one of the facts that

---

[11] See *Der Tagesspiegel,* 11 and 12 February 1970; Joachim Nawrocki, "Die Sowjets werden deutlich," *Die Zeit,* 13 February 1970; Hans B. Meyer, "Washington bleibt bereit zum Berlin-Gespräch," *Der Tagesspiegel,* 14 February 1970; *New York Times,* 11 and 12 February 1970.

[12] *New York Times,* 28 February 1970.

Bonn cannot alter," thereby indicating that the West German government was prepared to eventually recognize this situation as one of the realities of postwar Europe as long as the quadripartite status of Greater Berlin was not affected.[13]

Horst Ehmke, director of the office of the chancellor, sent the official West German response on behalf of Chancellor Brandt on 18 February. In a teletype message the chancellor accepted Chairman Stoph's invitation, welcomed "a start on normalization of the relationship of the two states in Germany . . . (as) a mutual contribution to relaxation and security in Europe," and suggested that the second meeting between the two leaders take place in Bonn.[14] Chancellor Brandt proposed that the technical arrangements for the meeting be discussed between representatives of both governments at the end of February in Berlin. These technical arrangements proved more difficult to negotiate than was expected in West Germany.

On 2 March Ulrich Sahm, ministerial director in the office of the chancellor, met in East Berlin with Gerhard Schüssler, deputy chief of the office of the Council of Ministers, to discuss the coming meeting between Chancellor Brandt and Chairman Stoph. Difficulties developed almost immediately. Although Sahm and his advisers had traveled to East Berlin through a checkpoint in the Berlin Wall, Schüssler demanded on behalf of the German Democratic Republic that the chancellor travel to the proposed meeting in East Berlin by rail—thereby avoiding West Berlin. The SED party organ, *Neues Deutschland,* wrote on 6 March that in the interests of the success of the forthcoming negotiations between the four powers on "West Berlin," the German Democratic Republic could not condone a violation of "international agreements." Therefore, Chancellor Brandt could not be allowed to proceed to the capital city of the German Democratic Republic from the "independent political entity" of West Berlin or to West Berlin from the German Democratic Republic. This position was initially confusing. East German officials had raised no objection in mid-1968 when Chancellor Brandt, in his capacity as foreign minister, came from West Berlin to visit Soviet Ambassador Abrasimov in the

---

[13] The text of Brandt's letter is reprinted in *Erfurt March 19, 1970: A Documentation* (Bonn: Press and Information Office of the Government of the Federal Republic of Germany, 1970). The press secretary's remarks can be found in *Die Welt,* 13 February 1970.

[14] *Erfurt March 19, 1970.*

Soviet sector. At that time the East German officials already considered West Berlin to be politically independent.[15]

The coming negotiations between East and West Germany, those on Berlin and the ongoing discussions between West Germany and Poland and West Germany and the Soviet Union, presented a different diplomatic situation. East Germany could now see a distinct political disadvantage for its negotiating position if West Germany could prove that East Germany had not objected to federal officials symbolically representing West Berlin. If East Germany wanted to argue that West Berlin was politically independent, it would be to its advantage to gain advance West German disavowal of any past occurrences that would otherwise support Western contentions. When West Germany proved adamant in maintaining the right of its officials to visit West Berlin in performance of their official duties and rejected the East German attempt to prescribe the route to be used by Chancellor Brandt, Chairman Stoph suggested that the meeting be held in Erfurt. This suggestion, according to Der Tagesspiegel, would cast the East Germans in the role of moderates advocating compromise.[16] It was uncertain whether this decision was an effort "to put what separates us into the background and to seek what links us," as Chancellor Brandt had urged.[17]

The decision was acceptable to Chancellor Brandt, but it was not necessarily an indication of East German or Soviet respect for the "good will" of the West German government which was the way columnist Dieter Cycon described it. According to Cycon, writing for the conservative West German daily Die Welt, the entire procedure suggested that the German Democratic Republic was less interested in détente than in improving its own and the Soviet position on West Berlin. Joachim Boelke, of the liberal West Berlin daily Der Tagesspiegel, interpreted the East German position as an attempt to gain West German acknowledgment that a visit by Chancellor Brandt to West Berlin was illegal and constituted a "provocation." Boelke had earlier predicted that the Western desire to ease tension in Berlin through negotiations with the Soviet Union would be rewarded with a demand

---

[15] Neues Deutschland, 6 March 1970; Die Welt, 3, 4, 5, 6 and 7 March 1970; Frankfurter Allgemeine Zeitung, 7 March 1970.

[16] See Der Tagesspiegel, 13 March 1970.

[17] Chancellor Brandt's 18 February letter to Chairman Stoph is also reprinted in Erfurt March 19, 1970.

for joint responsibility for the Western sectors of the city and in addition that East Germany and the Soviet Union would both seek to make West Germany's efforts to improve relations with Eastern Europe dependent on restricting political ties between the Federal Republic and West Berlin.[18]

The commentary in *Neues Deutschland,* the party organ of the SED, on 8 March tended to confirm Boelke's and Cycon's analyses. In the paper's editorial, the question of a proper meeting place was declared not to be a question of "West and East Berlin," but a question of "West Berlin, an independent political entity" and of "Berlin, the capital of the German Democratic Republic." As far as West Berlin was concerned, Chancellor Brandt had "nothing to seek there" since West Berlin was "not a state [Land] of the West German Federal Republic and may consequently not be governed by it."

The East German position clearly indicated, according to Boelke (one of the best informed political analysts in West Berlin), "that a policy of détente, as far as the real interests of both sides are concerned, is nothing else than the continuation of the cold war by other means: the same problems appear as before." Notwithstanding this continuation of the cold war, or perhaps commensurate with it, the East German government assured its citizens in March that the cold war was at an end—or that it would be at an end were it not for Chancellor Brandt's intention to jeopardize the four-power talks by creating a deliberate provocation with his visit to West Berlin.[19]

Both the East and West German governments hailed the decision to meet at Erfurt, and not Berlin, as a compromise. *Neues Deutschland* termed the decision a "renewed confirmation of the decisive and consistent policy of the German Democratic Republic toward assuring peace in Europe." To reinforce this statement the paper referred to endorsements of the East German compromise that appeared in newspapers in the Soviet Union, Poland, Sweden, Denmark, France, Belgium, Chile, Czechoslovakia, Hungary, Bulgaria, Algeria, the Sudan, and Mongolia.[20]

---

18 Dieter Cycon, "Das Vorspiel in Ost-Berlin," *Die Welt,* 7 March 1970; Joachim Boelke, "Ulbrichts Prioritäten," *Der Tagesspiegel,* 20 January 1970 and "Das Maximum," *Der Tagesspiegel,* 10 March 1970.

19 See the remarks of Joachim Herrmann, state secretary for West German questions, *Neues Deutschland,* 11 March 1970.

20 *Der Tagesspiegel,* 13 March 1970; *Neues Deutschland,* 15 March 1970.

The meeting in Erfurt took place on 19 March. Chancellor Brandt declared in his opening statement that agreements between the two governments could not affect or replace the four-power agreements concerning Germany and Berlin, nor could these agreements be affected by accords between West Germany and her allies or between East Germany and the Soviet Union. Specifically, the chancellor stated, ". . . we do not want to change the status of Berlin as long as the German question has not been resolved. I mean to say that one cannot, on the one hand, demand recognition of realities and on the other hand demand a one-sided alteration of the given situation." The chancellor emphasized that it was the responsibility of "the Four Powers to decide how they want to exercise their supreme authority in Berlin," and that the Federal Republic would welcome an agreement "reached among them on an improvement of the present situation." Chancellor Brandt stated the position of his government on the ties between West Berlin and the Federal Republic. He drew special attention to the point that "West Berlin is not distinguishable, economically, financially, juridically, and culturally" from West Germany. He placed stress on how "the fact that West Berlin is not governed by the Federation has not prevented the three powers from assigning to the Federal Government certain responsibilities, e.g., that of representing West Berlin abroad; again, that of concerning ourselves with the economic livelihood of the state [Land] of Berlin." In addition, he said, "neither the three Western powers, nor the FRG [Federal Republic of Germany], nor the directly affected Berliners would agree to any change in Berlin's status, as laid down by the Four Powers, that would lead to a change in these links." The chancellor concluded that for his government "efforts towards normalization and relaxation of tension in the center of Europe are inseparably connected with relaxation and normalization of the situation in and around Berlin." [21]

Chancellor Brandt's views on Berlin were not interpreted by Chairman Stoph to be in accord with "normalization and relaxation of tension in the center of Europe." Stoph denied that there existed "a Four-Power responsibility for the German Democratic Republic and its capital of Berlin . . . it is neither under Four-Power nor under Three-Power responsibility. The German Democratic Republic is an independent

---

[21] *Frankfurter Allgemeine Zeitung,* 20 March 1970. The English text is taken from *Erfurt March 19, 1970.*

sovereign Socialist state." [22] He proposed that the Federal Republic and the German Democratic Republic discuss the establishment of diplomatic relations using Ulbricht's draft treaty as a basis for discussion.

In a speech to the People's Chamber in East Berlin two days after the Erfurt meeting, Chairman Stoph repeated his demand for diplomatic recognition and reaffirmed his position on Berlin. He declared that "West Berlin does not belong to the Federal Republic and never will belong to it, but is instead an independent political unit in the midst of and on the territory of the German Democratic Republic." Consequently he called on the Federal Republic "to refrain from all activities that burden the situation in and around West Berlin . . . in view of the planned four-power negotiations on West Berlin and in consideration of the development of relations between the German Democratic Republic and the Federal Republic of Germany." He proposed that both states "should reach agreement on respecting West Berlin's status as an independent political unit, and, with this in mind, should regulate their relations with West Berlin" according to Article 7 of the draft treaty submitted to President Heinemann in December.[23]

The meeting between the two German leaders and their decision to continue discussions with a meeting scheduled for 21 May in Kassel, West Germany, introduced a new variable into the diplomatic equation. In addition, State Secretary Georg Ferdnand Dückwitz of the West German foreign office had already met with Polish officials to begin discussion of the Oder-Neisse line and arrangements for a renunciation of force agreement. State Secretary Egon Bahr of the chancellor's office was in the midst of discussions with Foreign Minister Gromyko on an agreement for mutual renunciation of force. Moreover, West Germany was consulting with France, Great Britain, and the United States on the coming quadripartite talks on Berlin. The Federal Republic would have to maintain a very careful differentiation between quadripartite responsibility for Berlin and Germany as a whole and West Germany's own responsibilities for improving intra-German and Eastern relations if the position of the Western powers on Berlin was not to be compromised. Chancellor Brandt did not want to reduce chances for German reunification by undermining existing quadripartite responsibilities for Germany. His task was complicated by the number of simultaneous proceedings and by the contradictions between Eastern

---

[22] *Neues Deutschland,* 20 March 1970.
[23] Ibid., 22 March 1970.

and Western positions.[24] The chancellor acknowledged that the prospect of German unity was remote. But without initiatives to improve the situation, the prospect for reunification would never be any less remote.

The East German position did not require differentiation between its talks with the Federal Republic and the quadripartite responsibilities for Berlin and Germany as a whole. The German Democratic Republic considered itself to be a sovereign state and wished to be treated as such. It considered Berlin to be its capital city, and indeed East Berlin is, for all practical purposes, its capital city. Thus it emphasized the existence of a "West Berlin" problem and the existence of a quadripartite status for that part of the city in which, according to Walter Ulbricht, it did not wish to interfere. Consequently East Germany and the Soviet Union pressed the following points before the opening of the quadripartite negotiations on Berlin: (1) West Berlin was not a "part" of the Federal Republic; (2) West Berlin was an "independent political entity" and the performance of specific official acts by West German government officials and their presence in West Berlin was therefore illegal; (3) the four-power status for Greater Berlin no longer applied to the Soviet sector; (4) the Soviet sector of Berlin was the capital and thus a part of the sovereign state of the German Democratic Republic; (5) the German Democratic Republic's government was responsible for granting access to and from the Soviet sector and East Germany; (6) the Soviet Union was a party to a quadripartite status for West Berlin; and (7) West Berlin could not be represented abroad by the Federal Republic.[25]

Analysis of the Negotiating Positions

The first round of position statements, from January to March, disclosed few if any common goals for Berlin. Neither side could easily recognize the other's position. The Western powers could offer few concessions that would not jeopardize their legal status in the city. The Soviet Union and East Germany, however, could give a great deal by merely rescinding the various measures undertaken to isolate the city.

---

[24] Joachim Boelke's editorial to the same effect, "Hebel und Regulativ," appeared in *Der Tagesspiegel,* 26 March 1970.

[25] Ferdinand Freidensburg, "Keine 'selbständige politische Einheit': Moskaus West-Berlin-Formel ist ohne jede Rechtsgrundlage," *Der Tagesspiegel,* 25 February 1970.

Thus, several possible compromises were conceivable, even though the positions were far apart.

The Soviet government could agree with *Zugang*, unrestricted access to West Berlin, without threatening the stability of the East German government. The Western powers could restrict West German federal presence in West Berlin in exchange for *Zugang*. However, the West would have to make certain that a reduction in West German federal presence based on an acknowledgment that West Berlin was not a "constituent" part of the Federal Republic was not the beginning of further isolation of West Berlin. The elimination of harassment would make travel easier and residence in West Berlin much more attractive. This compromise would be particularly desirable if the Soviet government granted *Zuordnung*, the recognition of West Berlin's legal, cultural, and financial ties with West Germany, together with *Zugang*. Such a recognition would not mean that the city was a "constituent" part of the Bundesrepublik, only that such ties as already existed should be maintained and developed. The eventual reduction of federal presence was a compromise the West could make since West Berlin had never been a "constituent" part of West Germany in a legal sense.

Soviet agreement to the principle of *Zuordnung* would represent acknowledgment of a condition existing since the creation of the Federal Republic in 1949. It would not jeopardize any Soviet position. In such a bargain the West could implicitly acknowledge East Berlin's ties with East Germany and, consequently, the function of the Soviet sector as the capital of the GDR. Such an acknowledgment would also be recognition of a condition existing since 1949.

A Soviet grant of *Zutritt*, giving West Berliners the same access to East Berlin and East Germany as West Germans enjoyed, in exchange for Western recognition of East Berlin, would not be acceptable. A grant of *Zutritt* would not be a concession because its denial was a direct violation of existing four-power agreements. However, a Soviet decision to grant *Zugang*, *Zuordnung*, and *Zutritt* without gaining diplomatic recognition would represent a compromise.

While the question of according the GDR diplomatic recognition could not be the subject of the quadripartite negotiations, the Federal Republic had made future progress of the intra-German discussions, which might lead to diplomatic relations of some kind in the future, dependent on conclusion of a satisfactory Berlin agreement. In turn, the establishment in the future of some form of diplomatic representation between the GDR and the Federal Republic in East Berlin and Bonn would presumably presage the diplomatic recognition of the GDR by other Western nations, possibly including France, Great Britain, and the United States. Therefore, the questions of sovereignty and diplomatic recognition for the GDR were indirectly related to possible quadripartite compromises and concessions on the Berlin problem.

Just prior to the first meeting of the four ambassadors on 26 March, West Berlin's mayor, Klaus Schütz, referring to some of these considerations, once again warned of the difficulty of the negotiations. He pointed out that an alteration in the status of the city would be unacceptable. He added that those who ignored West Berlin's legal, economic and financial ties to the Federal Republic endangered the political climate in Europe and incurred the risk of losing their credibility when speaking of peace and understanding.[26] The German Democratic Republic did not increase the credibility of its assurances that its policies were guided by peace when its border patrol shot a refugee at the Berlin Wall on 22 March.

The continual attention paid to the issue of West Berlin's ties with the Bundesrepublik and the issue of federal presence in West Berlin reflected their true importance. Chancellor Brandt himself stressed the integrity of West Germany's ties with West Berlin several days before the beginning of the quadripartite negotiations. He emphasized that the federal government was prepared to acknowledge existing conditions, presumably in an effort to indicate that the West was prepared to compromise. He declared that "the actual competence" for control of the Berlin autobahns rested with the East German officials to whom he had shown his papers and paid his fees as the mayor of Berlin. He added that "Allied competence was valid in a very narrow sense and there mainly for military personnel." [27]

These assertions and rejections and the emphasis on existing conditions and détente contained in the statements of Eastern and Western leaders prior to the first quadripartite meeting serve as an introduction to the issues to be negotiated for the next eighteen months. And while this presentation may have seemed unnecessarily repetitious, it does reflect the gradual clarification of negotiating positions which President

[26] *Die Welt,* 23 March 1970.

[27] *Frankfurter Allgemeine Zeitung,* 25 March 1970.

Nixon believed was necessary. Each round of the exchange brought a little more clarity. The result was that when the first quadripartite meeting took place on 26 March, each side could see the difficulties inherent in the coming negotiations. But by no means was any final agreement certain.

3
The Negotiations: The First Year

The first quadripartite meeting on Berlin was convened on 26 March 1970. Excitement and optimism accompanied the opening session. The parliamentary floor leader of the Free Democratic Party (FDP) in the Bundestag, Wolfgang Mischnik, considered the discussions on Berlin to be a touchstone for relations between the states of divided Europe. The former chancellor, Kurt Georg Kiesinger, viewed them as a test case that would indicate the good will of the East.[1] The Polish television network commented that "there are possibilities West Berlin could play a decisive role in détente between East and West, if the Western side shows understanding for the realities." [2] This last theme, the idea that all would be well if only the West would understand the "realities" of the situation was also sounded by East Germany. As a good will gesture on 26 March the West had suspended the activities of the Allied Travel Office (ATO) in West Berlin.[3] *Neues Deutschland*

---

[1] *Die Welt,* 28 March 1970.

[2] Ibid., 29 March 1970.

[3] See Joachim Boelke, "Der Beginn," *Der Tagesspiegel,* 27 March 1970 and *Neues Deutschland,* 27 March 1970. The Allied Travel Office was established in 1946 as an organ of the Allied Control Council for the purpose of issuing a "temporary travel document" to German citizens who wished to travel outside Germany. In 1952 the three Western powers gave the West German government the authority to issue its own passports. Thereafter, the ATO, located in the former Allied Control Council building in the American sector of Berlin, was only responsible for issuing these travel documents to citizens of East Berlin and East Germany who wished to visit Western countries. They were required to have one of these documents before the Western country they wished to visit would grant them a visa. The German Democratic Republic claimed that this procedure violated its sovereignty as well as the sovereignty of the Western states which had to wait for the travel document before issuing a visa. By 1970 there was considerable

saw the closure not as a good will gesture, but as the consequence of "the hard pressure of realities." [4]

The quadripartite negotiations were slow and laborious. The first six meetings dealt with procedural detail and the formal establishment of negotiating positions.[5] Since the progress of the quadripartite negotiations on Berlin was not rapid, public attention returned to the intra-German discussions and the Soviet-West German negotiations.

Second Intra-German Discussion: Kassel

Chancellor Brandt and Chairman Stoph met in Kassel, West Germany, on 21 May, one week after the third quadripartite meeting on Berlin. At the meeting they discussed Berlin and its connection with the Federal Republic's efforts to improve East-West relations. Chancellor Brandt set forth twenty points expressing the Federal Republic's view on the "principles and elements of the treaty regularizing relations between the Federal Republic of Germany and the German Democratic Republic on terms of equality." These principles expanded the points the chancellor had presented in his 14 January address to the Bundestag and had repeated at the first meeting at Erfurt.

Although Chancellor Brandt was not prepared to accord the German Democratic Republic diplomatic recognition as a sovereign state, he did propose that both leaders "respect the independence and autonomy of each of the two States in affairs affecting their internal sovereign authority." In addition to supporting an expansion of trade, the chancellor proposed an extension of cooperation in the spheres of transportation and traffic, postal communications and telecommunications, science, education, culture, environmental problems, and athletics. He specifically emphasized the necessity for both states to observe and acknowledge the rights and responsibilities of the four powers for Berlin and for Germany as a whole, as well as the necessity for them to respect past quadripartite agreements and "the ties which have developed between West Berlin and the Federal Republic of Germany."

---

criticism of the ATO by many governments, particularly the Scandinavian governments. See *The Allied Travel Office (ATO) in West Berlin: Illegal Obstruction on the Road to the Guarantee of European Security* (Dresden: Verlag Zeit im Bild, 1970).

[4] *Neues Deutschland,* 28 and 29 March 1970.

[5] See *Der Tagesspiegel,* 29 April, 7, 14 and 15 May 1970, and *Neue Zürcher Zeitung,* 29 April 1970.

He concluded his remarks by saying that "progress . . . towards securing a normalization of the situation in and around Berlin would also be of importance for the further continuance of the discussions between our two Governments." [6]

As he had at Erfurt, Chairman Stoph demanded diplomatic recognition of the German Democratic Republic as a sovereign state, recognition of the Oder-Neisse line and of the border dividing East and West Germany, and admission of both German states to the United Nations. He proposed once more that the draft treaty submitted to the Federal Republic in December 1969 provide the basis for negotiations. The East German position on Berlin had not changed. Chairman Stoph declared that "it is universally well-known that the independent political entity West Berlin, which is situated in the middle of the German Democratic Republic and on her territory, was not, and whatever happens never will be, a part of the Federal Republic of Germany." Stoph rejected "all attempts by the government of the Federal Republic of Germany to interfere in West Berlin affairs," and asserted that the Federal Republic "possesses no rights or competencies whatever in and for West Berlin." He said further that "the settlement of the problem of West Berlin and the establishment of international relations" between the German Democratic Republic and the Federal Republic of Germany were unconnected issues.

Chancellor Brandt disagreed with the East German position on the connection between the intra-German discussions and the quadripartite negotiations. He declared in a press conference following the meeting that "an evaluation of the Kassel conference must not be undertaken in isolation; the meeting must be considered within the broader framework," including not only the quadripartite negotiations on Berlin, but also the Federal Republic's negotiations with the Soviet Union and Poland.

The East Germans were understandably loath to accept the chancellor's framework because he appeared to be making a compromise on recognition dependent on support by both German states for the quadripartite negotiations. Chairman Ulbricht did not wish recognition by West Germany at the expense of the East German claim to sovereignty

---

[6] The text of the chancellor's remarks is contained in *Kassel, May 21, 1970: A Documentation* (Bonn: Press and Information Office of the Government of the Federal Republic of Germany, 1970). Chairman Stoph's reply is also printed in this book.

in Berlin and authority over the city's access routes. However, his declaration in January that progress on an intra-German agreement for renunciation of force was dependent on the outcome of the negotiations for such an agreement between West Germany and the Soviet Union suggested that he too had a framework within which he evaluated the Kassel meeting.[7]

Chancellor Brandt and Chairman Stoph did not agree on a date for a third meeting, but both leaders expressed the hope that a further exchange of views would take place after each government had considered its position. As June and July passed there were strong indications that both governments would await progress on Berlin and the talks between the Soviet Union and the Federal Republic before resuming discussions.

Treaty between West Germany and the Soviet Union

On 7 August Foreign Ministers Gromyko and Scheel initialed a Soviet-West German treaty. Chancellor Brandt and Premier Kosygin signed it on 12 August. The treaty provided for a mutual renunciation of force and established that existing conditions in Europe would be used as the basis for all future negotiations. The West German government recognized all European borders as inviolable, including the Oder-Neisse line and the border dividing East and West Germany. In their communiqué on 13 August, the Soviet and West German governments declared that "the Treaty will further the strengthening of security in Europe, the solutions of the problems existing there and the realization of a peaceful cooperation among all European states irrespective of the differences in their social order."

Chancellor Brandt considered the completion of the Soviet-West German treaty as a major step toward diminishing tension between West Germany and the Soviet Union and between Eastern and Western Europe in general. He also believed that the treaty would contribute to the conclusion of a satisfactory Berlin agreement. In his televised address to the German people, delivered from Moscow on 12 August, the chancellor sought to dispel any suspicion in West Germany or among the Federal Republic's allies that his government would make unilateral concessions to the Soviet Union. He stressed that "it accords

---

[7] *Der Tagesspiegel,* 18 July 1970.

with the interests of the entire German people to improve relations with the Soviet Union in particular. Not only is she one of the major World Powers; she also shares in the special responsibility for Germany as a whole and Berlin." He went on to say that "tomorrow it will be nine years since the Wall was built. Today we have—I confidently hope—made a start in order to counteract the rift, in order that people will no longer have to die in barbed wire, until the day comes when—so we hope—the division of our people can be overcome." He concluded by saying that the treaty did not weaken in any way the Federal Republic's firm inclusion in the Atlantic Alliance, her partnerships with the United States and France, or her determination to work towards the goal of eventual political unity in Europe.[8]

In identical notes on 7 August, the Federal Republic had assured the three Western powers that quadripartite rights and responsibilities for Germany as a whole and for Berlin were not affected by the treaty, and that the Soviet government was in agreement on this point. In a press conference in Bonn on 14 August, Chancellor Brandt reiterated his position that "the Western Alliance is not weakened but strengthened by a concerted policy of détente." He emphasized that the treaty was a joint contribution "for a more satisfactory state of affairs in Europe" similar to the efforts of the United States and the Soviet Union to limit strategic weapons. In addition, he expected that "improved relations" between the Soviet Union and the Federal Republic "will not have an unfavorable effect on the idea of a European conference on questions of security and possibly other issues." He believed the treaty would "assist the discussions of the Four Powers directed towards reaching a satisfactory settlement of affairs in and around Berlin." He stated also that he expected "decisive progress" in the negotiations with Poland in the next month, and he hoped that discussions with the GDR could be continued by experts of both governments.

In their response to the chancellor's letter (11 August), the three Western powers concurred that because a German peace settlement was yet to be made, quadripartite rights and responsibilities for Berlin and Germany remained unaffected. In Washington a State Department

---

[8] The texts of the Soviet-West German treaty, of Chancellor Brandt's remarks, and all associated documents, letters, and press conferences are contained in *The Treaty of August 12, 1970 between the Federal Republic of Germany and the Union of the Soviet Socialist Republics* (Bonn: Press and Information Office of the Government of the Federal Republic of Germany, 1970).

spokesman declared that the United States endorsed West German efforts to improve its relations with the Soviet Union and Eastern Europe and hoped that the Soviet Union would contribute to improving the Berlin situation.[9]

Chancellor Brandt's assurances notwithstanding, the CDU/CSU bloc feared that a stated progress towards détente was illusory. During the summer the CDU/CSU had warned that Brandt's negotiating tactics would only perpetuate the division of Germany, preserve the status quo in Europe, and ultimately contribute to the diplomatic recognition of the GDR.[10] They viewed the recognition of European borders as a unilateral Western concession. They feared that this would weaken any remaining chance that Germany could be reunited. Foreign Minister Scheel's letter to Foreign Minister Gromyko stating that the treaty did not conflict with the West German government's position on unification according to self-determination was believed to be inadequate.[11]

As if to confirm CDU/CSU suspicions that East Germany would try to exploit any efforts of the federal government to improve relations with Eastern Europe, Secretary Ulbricht stated that the recognition of the German border was tacit recognition of East Germany and immediately called for diplomatic recognition.[12] Rainer Barzel, parliamentary floor leader for the CDU, addressed a letter to Chancellor Brandt to this effect on 10 August. Barzel wrote that the CDU/CSU agreed with the federal government that negotiations with Poland, East Germany, and the Soviet Union, and the quadripartite negotiations on Berlin were to be seen as a whole. They agreed that the Soviet-West German treaty should not be enacted until a satisfactory Berlin agreement had been achieved. But, he wrote, the CDU/CSU could not approve the Soviet treaty until the other negotiations had also produced acceptable agreements, especially agreements on Berlin and relations between the Germanys. Moreover, there were other potential problems. The CDU/CSU, and on this matter the SPD-FDP coalition, suspected that the Soviet-West German treaty would weaken the American desire to maintain troops in Europe. This was substantiated on 23 August. Senators Fulbright, Young, and Mansfield of the Senate Foreign Rela-

---

9 *Die Welt,* 14 August 1970.

10 Ibid., 22, 23 and 25 through 29 May; 1, 2, 5, 6, 8, 11, 15 and 26 June; 2, 4, 17, 24, 25, 27, 28 and 31 July; 1, 3, 5, 6 and 7 August 1970.

11 Ibid., 12 through 15 August 1970.

12 *Neues Deutschland,* 9 through 15 August 1970.

tions Committee declared that the United States should reduce its troops on the continent to a "symbolic contingent" of 50,000 since the Soviet Union and West Germany had successfully reduced tension on the continent.[13]

The *Junktim*

Earlier in July, Foreign Minister Scheel had argued that the Soviet Union could not logically sign an agreement for mutual renunciation of force while pursuing a deliberate policy of tension in Berlin.[14] During the Bundestag debate on the Soviet-West German treaty on 18 September, Chancellor Brandt returned to this theme. He declared that a relaxation of tension in Europe would be impossible without improvements on the Berlin question. The chancellor stated that in view of the connection between Berlin and European tension, West Germany could not ratify the treaty with the Soviet Union until a satisfactory Berlin agreement had been reached.[15] This connection was rapidly referred to in the West German press as the *Junktim*.

Chancellor Brandt emphasized that this *Junktim* was understood in Moscow. Thus the Soviet attempt a week later to close the Berlin air corridors temporarily, ostensibly for technical reasons, caused considerable concern in West Germany and among the Western Allies. A Soviet journalist, Juri Schukov, a member of the Foreign Policy Committee of the Supreme Soviet, did not lessen this concern with his remarks while visiting Bonn that September. Schukov said that Berlin was the capital city of the German Democratic Republic, while West Berlin was a third part of Germany under four-power control. He did, however, acknowledge its economic and financial connections with the Federal Republic. The CDU/CSU criticized these remarks as an indication that the Soviet government still sought to undermine the four-power status of Berlin despite its endorsement of détente and peaceful coexistence. Press Secretary Ahlers, expressing the official West German position, pointed out that the Soviet Union understandably did not wish to indicate its final negotiating position before the four-power

---

[13] *Die Welt,* 11, 14 and 24 August 1970.

[14] Walter Scheel, "Die deutsche Politik des Gewaltverzichts," *Frankfurter Allgemeine Zeitung,* 15 July 1970.

[15] Ibid., 19 September and 23 October 1970.

discussions had concluded. The West German government would await developments in the Berlin negotiations scheduled to resume on 30 September.[16]

Following the September quadripartite meeting, and possibly in connection with Schukov's remarks on Berlin, several officials in West Berlin and West Germany speculated on the possibility that an eventual agreement would increase "Soviet responsibility" in the Western sectors. This encouraged rumors that following a Berlin agreement the Soviet Union might reoccupy the building it owned on Lietzenburger Strasse in the American sector in order to establish a trade mission. The question of increased Soviet presence in West Berlin was an especially sensitive one because of past Soviet and East German assertions that West Berlin was an "independent political entity" existing under four-power status. This claim had been sharply rejected by the Western powers in the past. But West German opinion was divided on its significance. The West German government maintained that if a mutually acceptable agreement could be achieved by allowing increased Soviet presence, then whatever detriments such presence might bring could well be outweighed by the overall effects of the treaty.[17]

A writer for the *Frankfurter Allgemeine Zeitung* delineated the changes in opinion and the pressures for compromise that the negotiations were beginning to create. He suggested that some West German officials, whom he did not name, believed an agreement depended upon a more conciliatory Western attitude. It was perplexing to many in West Germany, he said, that apparently several of these officials, who had once been very critical of past Soviet policy on Berlin, now suggested that it was the West's cold war attitude which made compromise impossible.[18]

Foreign Minister Gromyko's views on the negotiations, expressed after the eighth quadripartite session in October, were similar to those which concerned the *Frankfurter Allgemeine Zeitung*. He declared that a "positive" outcome of the negotiations depended upon more than the good will of all participants. The decisive influence, he believed,

[16] *Frankfurter Allgemeine Zeitung,* 26, 28 and 29 September and 5 October 1970; *Pravda,* 4 October 1970.

[17] *Frankfurter Allgemeine Zeitung,* 2 October 1970.

[18] See Alfred Rapp, "Bonn von Moskau gedrängt," ibid., 9 October 1970, and Gunther Gillessen, "Das Junktim," ibid., 23 October 1970.

would be the West German adoption of a "more realistic attitude" toward the Berlin situation. Immediately after Gromyko's remarks, West German spokesmen emphasized that progress had been made in the seventh and eighth meetings on 30 September and 9 October. Chancellor Brandt again drew attention to the *Junktim:* the treaty would not be ratified unless there was a satisfactory agreement on Berlin.[19]

Ambassador Abrasimov reportedly reversed the Soviet position at the tenth quadripartite meeting on 16 November. At the ninth meeting on 4 November he had spoken of the willingness of his government to improve access to and from Berlin. But now he insisted upon East German sovereignty over the access routes and proposed that a separate access agreement be concluded between West and East Germany. The Western Allies sought an agreement on Berlin including *Zugang, Zuordnung,* and *Zutritt.* Abrasimov proposed that three separate agreements be concluded on these points and that West Germany should end its presence in West Berlin. France, Great Britain and the United States argued on the contrary that an intra-German agreement "must remain on a level well below a four-power agreement." To protect the Western position that the German Democratic Republic was not a sovereign state and that the Soviet government retained its responsibilities for access to and from Berlin, the West German government had declined to begin negotiations with the East German government until instructed to do so by the four powers themselves.[20]

At the same time, however, State Secretaries Egon Bahr of the Federal Republic and Michael Kohl of the German Democratic Republic met for the first of fifteen intra-German discussions on 27 November. This represented the continuation of the meetings held between Chancellor Brandt and Chairman Stoph earlier in 1970. The East Germans proposed, in agreement with the Soviet position presented to the Western powers on 16 November, that the intra-German discussions center on problems of access to and from Berlin on the East German highways. Because the West German government was anxious for the Berlin negotiations to produce an agreement as rapidly as possible, it was prepared to conduct exploratory discussions with the East German government on intra-German relations. With the groundwork thus prepared the GDR and the Federal Republic would be in a

---

[19] Ibid., 23 and 24 October 1970.
[20] See the *New York Times,* 17 November 1970.

position to conclude negotiations swiftly should the four powers empower them to do so.

By discussing problems of access to Berlin the German Democratic Republic hoped to undermine the quadripartite talks. If West Germany were to conclude an agreement on Berlin with East Germany, it would validate the 1955 Bolz-Zorin agreement according to which the German Democratic Republic was a sovereign state. West Germany, by waiting for specific instructions from the four powers to discuss an agreement with East Germany, maintained Soviet responsibility for unimpeded access to and from Berlin. For this reason Secretary Bahr was charged by his government to limit his discussions to general questions of East-West relations and to reject any East German overture to negotiate issues that were subjects of discussion at the quadripartite negotiations.

The problem of how to negotiate with East Germany also confronted the West Berlin Senat, whose representatives began preparatory talks with the East German government four months later on access for West Berliners to East Germany and East Berlin. In October and November 1970, the East Germans maintained that because West Berlin was an independent political entity, discussions concerning traffic questions between West Berlin and the German Democratic Republic would have to be conducted by the West Berlin Senat and the East German government. This would not, according to *Neues Deutschland,* prevent discussions between West Germany and East Germany, which were begun on 27 November, if West Germany adopted a "realistic and constructive" attitude.[21] It was believed in West Germany that the East Germans, with or without Soviet approval, sought to drive a wedge between the Western powers and the West German government. The East Germans, it was further believed, wished to create differences of opinion over the nature of the intra-German discussions before the four powers empowered the two German governments to conclude agreements. If the German Democratic Republic was successful, it would almost certainly have asserted that the Soviet government was relieved of all responsibility for traffic to and from Berlin. This would, of course, have altered the framework in which negotiations could be conducted. Therefore the governments of both West Germany and West Berlin were careful to emphasize throughout the talks that dis-

---

[21] *Neues Deutschland,* 5 November 1970.

cussions with their East German counterparts could not interfere with or impinge upon the four-power negotiations.[22]

Two days after the first meeting between Secretaries Bahr and Kohl in East Berlin, Secretary Brezhnev repeated the Soviet position in a speech in Erivan. The secretary declared that a healthier climate in Europe and with it an agreement on Berlin were feasible. To achieve these would require only that "all interested parties show good will and design solutions that acknowledge the wishes of the West Berlin population and observe the legitimate interests and sovereign rights of the German Democratic Republic." West German Deputy Press Secretary Rüdiger von Wechmar interpreted Brezhnev's speech as an indication that a Berlin agreement was certainly possible.[23] But Secretary Brezhnev's remarks raised two important questions: how did the Soviet Union interpret the wishes of the West Berlin population and how did the Soviet Union interpret the legitimate interests and sovereign rights of the GDR? These two questions led in turn to two more: did the interests of the GDR correspond with those of the Soviet Union in Berlin and was the East German government in a sufficiently strong position to interfere with access to West Berlin without Soviet approval?

It is difficult to answer these questions. Certainly no definitive answer can be supplied on the matter of Soviet intentions for West Berlin and East Germany. As long as the Western Allies rejected demands that the East and West German governments conclude all necessary agreements, the East German government could not be sure whether the Soviet Union would compromise on access in order to conclude an agreement and thereby gain West German ratification of the 12 August treaty. But even if the East Germans were concerned with Soviet intent, it would be highly unlikely the GDR would harass traffic in an attempt to prevent Soviet acceptance of a specific compromise. It is much more likely that the GDR was responsible for seeing generally that as few compromises as possible would have to be made. The more difficult it was to get to West Berlin, the more content the West would presumably

---

[22] See, for example, Rüdiger von Wechmar's remarks in the *Frankfurter Allgemeine Zeitung,* 23 November 1970. See also Dettmar Cramer, "Über die Zugangswege nach Berlin," ibid., 28 October 1970 for additional statements on the risks involved if the German Democratic Republic's efforts proved successful. See also the editorial by N. B. [presumably Nicholas Benckiser], ibid., 2 November 1970.

[23] The text of Brezhnev's speech is reprinted in *Neues Deutschland,* 30 November 1970, *Frankfurter Allgemeine Zeitung,* 1 December 1970, and *Der Tagesspiegel,* 1 and 2 December 1970.

be with any agreement providing at least some assurance of access. This would explain the conjecture in West Germany of Soviet "flexibility" and East German "intransigence." Nevertheless, some political observers in the Federal Republic, putting Secretary Ulbricht's cancellation of his state visit to Rumania and his absence at the Hungarian Communist party congress together with the traffic harassment at the end of November, concluded that Ulbricht was seeking "to show Mr. Brezhnev that East Germany is against making concessions to the West over Berlin, and that he deplores the whole trend of Mr. Brezhnev's *Westpolitik.*" [24]

During this period there were indications that East Germany's allies wished to improve their relations with the West, even though their support for diplomatic recognition of East Germany had not yet produced results. A Polish-West German treaty containing a mutual renunciation of force agreement and recognition of the Oder-Neisse line was initialed in November. The Czechoslovakian government indicated that it too wished to open negotiations with West Germany.

While it may be erroneous to conclude that there was in any sense a movement on the part of the East for genuine rapprochement, the *Junktim* was beginning to show signs of producing compromise. More than just the ratification of the Soviet-West Germany treaty had been made dependent upon a Berlin agreement. Foreign Minister Scheel suggested that the Polish-West German treaty could only be ratified if there was an acceptable Berlin agreement. In addition the NATO ministers agreed in December 1970 that the precondition for their support of a European security conference would be a satisfactory conclusion of the Berlin negotiations.

Demonstrative Federal Presence

Traffic harassment at the end of November seems to have been a response to the display of federal presence in Berlin: the CDU/CSU held a party caucus in the city. The resulting harassment lasted from 28 November until 2 December, with access delays of up to seventeen hours. Both the East German and the Soviet press assured their readers that the exercise of demonstrative presence reflected the intention of

---

[24] *Economist,* 5 December 1970, pp. 14-15. See also the *New York Times,* 1 December 1970 and *Le Monde,* 2 December 1970.

the "enemies of détente" to complicate the Berlin negotiations.[25] It was uncertain whether the Soviet government approved this particular display of sovereignty.

Mayor Schütz declared that this response was a return to the cold war. In Bonn, however, the SPD-FDP coalition questioned if the CDU/CSU meeting was not an attempt to provoke the East Germans, drawing attention to the difficulties of détente and Chancellor Brandt's Ostpolitik. The CDU/CSU maintained that this was not their intent but that they wished to demonstrate West Berlin's ties with the Federal Republic. Deputy Press Secretary von Wechmar declared on 30 November that while the government agreed such meetings could be held in West Berlin, it was another question whether it was wise to demonstrate federal presence with the negotiations in their current state. Rainer Barzel, parliamentary floor leader for the CDU, announced that the West German government had tried to discourage the CDU/CSU from holding the meeting in Berlin. He declared that it was the federal government's objection to the meeting and not the meeting itself which jeopardized the Berlin talks. Willi Bäuerle, a member of the SPD in the Bundestag, rejoined that the CDU/CSU by holding the meeting in Berlin had attacked the government "in the rear" while the chancellor was continuing his efforts to conduct Ostpolitik successfully.[26]

Whether the CDU/CSU meeting was unwise at that juncture in the negotiations is questionable. The meeting did show that the CDU/ CSU and presumably the West German government viewed federal presence as a right which it could continue to exercise until a satisfactory Berlin settlement was reached. But the deputy press secretary's remarks placed the West German government on record as being reluctant to exercise these rights. This reluctance was criticized by the CDU/CSU because it could be interpreted by the Soviet Union and the German Democratic Republic as an invitation to harass traffic under any similar circumstances in order to gain a unilateral concession from the West. If federal presence in West Berlin was to be used as a bargaining counter in the negotiations, the CDU/CSU argued, it had to be used regularly

---

[25] *Pravda,* 6 December 1970.

[26] Willi Bäuerle's remarks are reprinted in *Der Tagesspiegel,* 1 December 1970. Barzel's remarks were reported by the *Deutsche Presse Agentur* in Hamburg on 1 December 1970. See also *Der Tagesspiegel,* 1 and 2 December 1970; *Frankfurter Allgemeine Zeitung,* 2 December 1970; *New York Times,* 1 December 1970.

to retain its effectiveness.[27] The interference, whether or not it had Soviet backing, also served as a reminder that the border checkpoints were under de facto East German control and that should a quadripartite agreement be reached, at least the details would have to be worked out between East and West German officials.

Shortly after this exchange former Secretary of State Dean Acheson severely criticized Chancellor Brandt's conduct of Ostpolitik. In a White House meeting with President Nixon, Acheson said he believed that the chancellor's "mad race to Moscow" had to be slowed down if Berlin's status was not to be compromised. Since the success of Ostpolitik depended to such a great extent upon a Berlin settlement, Acheson was concerned that Chancellor Brandt would "settle for too little" in order to gain an agreement.[28] On 12 December Chancellor Brandt reaffirmed his position that an acceptable Berlin agreement would be the decisive test for the success of his efforts to decrease tension in Europe.[29] But it was precisely the importance of achieving a Berlin agreement that concerned Acheson. As he saw it, the chancellor needed the agreement not only to preserve his foreign policy but also to preserve his twelve-vote majority in the Bundestag. On 19 December, Acheson emphasized again that the chancellor's efforts to make rapid progress toward détente in order to preserve the SPD-FDP coalition could result in an unacceptable compromise on Berlin, jeopardizing the Western position in the city.[30]

On the same day that Acheson voiced his concerns over Ostpolitik, the West German government reversed its position on the exercise of federal presence in Berlin. Just three weeks after Deputy Press Secretary von Wechmar had suggested that the CDU/CSU meeting was inadvisable, the SPD held a party meeting in Berlin. Traffic interference began on 19 December and ceased on 22 December. The Soviet news agency Tass reported on 21 December that "cold war advocates" were attempting to thwart "the growing desire of the people of Europe for

---

27 See *Der Tagesspiegel* and *Frankfurter Allgemeine Zeitung*, 1 through 5 December 1970.

28 Also attending the meeting were John J. McCloy, former ambassador to the Federal Republic, Lucius D. Clay, former high commissioner in Germany, and Thomas E. Dewey. See Chalmers Roberts, "Acheson Urges Brandt's 'Race' to Moscow Be 'Cooled Off,' " *Washington Post,* 10 December 1970.

29 *Der Tagesspiegel,* 13 December 1970.

30 *New York Times,* 20 December 1970.

détente" and were conducting a campaign with "the sole purpose of causing international complications." Whether the SPD's decision to hold a meeting in Berlin was made to stem criticism in the United States over the conduct of Ostpolitik is uncertain. It is certain that West German officials, most of whom belonged to the SPD, were concerned by the American criticism. The federal government expressed the hope on 19 December that a rift was not developing between Bonn and Washington.

The official Washington position supported West Germany. On 21 December State Department spokesman Robert McCloskey denied the existence of a "crisis of confidence" between the United States and the Federal Republic. The American government, he said, supported Chancellor Brandt's efforts to improve relations with his East European neighbors. McCloskey declared that the Soviet Union bore the "preponderant responsibility" for the harassment and that it called into question the sincerity of the Soviet desire to bring about improvements in the city. On the same day Press Secretary Ahlers assured newsmen in Bonn that complete harmony existed between Bonn and Washington on the subject of Berlin.[31]

In the middle of December, believing that negotiations had reached an impasse, Chancellor Brandt sent notes to the French, British, and United States governments urging that the four-power talks be accelerated. He suggested the formation of a permanent committee consisting of four-power representatives just under the rank of ambassador to discuss the Berlin problem. Since the twelfth meeting had been held on 10 December and the thirteenth was not scheduled until 19 January, the proposal merited consideration from his point of view. The *Frankfurter Allgemeine Zeitung* cautioned that should the chancellor's office attempt to exert pressure on the Western powers, thereby betraying anxiety that an agreement might not be reached, such efforts would be interpreted by the GDR and the Soviet governments as an indication of weakness.[32] In addition, it would reflect the growing concern of the SPD to CDU/CSU criticism in the wake of autobahn harassment. When Secretaries Bahr and Kohl met in East Berlin on 23 December, the CDU/CSU objected that Bonn was negotiating under pressure. They pointed out that if this was indeed the case, the Soviet Union

---

[31] Both men's remarks are in the *New York Times,* 22 December 1970.
[32] *Frankfurter Allgemeine Zeitung,* 28 December 1970.

could be expected to prolong negotiations in the hopes of gaining more concessions as pressure mounted.[33]

Time was an important factor, for the continuance of the negotiations allowed more and more criticism, which in turn placed more and more pressure on the coalition. As Acheson had pointed out and as Chancellor Brandt was aware, the governing coalition enjoyed a majority of only twelve seats in the Bundestag. This meant that should criticism of his conduct of Ostpolitik mount to a point where six Social Democrats or Free Democrats were to switch and join the CDU/CSU on a vote, the parliamentary draw would require the Bundestag to be dissolved and new elections to be held.[34] Acheson believed that fear of such a situation accounted for part of Chancellor Brandt's concern that the negotiations not be stalemated and for the consistent professions of optimism from the office of the chancellor. On his behalf, Chancellor Brandt hoped that his moves towards unblocking the negotiations would shift the onus of procrastination to the Soviet Union, even though Premier Kosygin accused the Western powers of procrastination in his 1971 New Year's message.[35] Thus, Chancellor Brandt continued to draw special emphasis to his government's firm position in an effort to reassure his allies that West Germany was not prepared to endorse unacceptable compromise on Berlin.

January and February 1971

To usher in the new year, both Chancellor Brandt and Herbert Wehner, the parliamentary floor leader for the Social Democratic Party, expressed optimism that an acceptable agreement would be concluded that year. Mayor Schütz, revising earlier predictions, decided that it would be apparent by the summer whether an agreement was in the offing.[36]

A few days later Herbert Wehner attacked the *Junktim*, declaring that failure to conclude the treaty with the Soviet Union would be a "disaster for German policy." [37] He argued that West Germany could

---

[33] Ibid., 24 and 28 through 31 December 1970.

[34] The 1972 federal elections were held following a parliamentary stalemate brought about by members switching parties.

[35] Tass, 2 January 1971. See also the *New York Times,* 20 December 1970.

[36] *Frankfurter Allgemeine Zeitung,* 2 and 5 January 1971; *Relay from Bonn,* 8 January 1971.

[37] *Frankfurter Allgemeine Zeitung,* 5 and 6 January 1971.

reduce East German pressure by letting the Soviet treaty ride on its own merits. In so doing West Germany would prove to East Germany that the GDR could not impede the progress of détente. Wehner made two assumptions, one implicit and one explicit. Implicitly he assumed that East Germany alone was responsible for interference with access to West Berlin, although commentaries in *Pravda* as well as statements by Tass had indicated that the Soviet Union fully supported the harassment of December. Explicitly, he maintained that East Germany was concerned with the possible effects détente would have on the ideological commitment of its citizens. This was valid. He argued that the East German government was harassing the access ways because it had little confidence in the ideological commitment of its citizens. By its harassment, he said, East Germany sought to delay or prevent the Berlin agreement and, as long as the *Junktim* lasted, the Soviet agreement as well. Hence West Germany should dissolve the *Junktim.* Otherwise the Federal Republic might not be considered an "equal partner in the struggle for peace" in Europe. He did not specify who might not consider West Germany to be an equal partner, but implied that the step toward détente represented by the Soviet and Polish treaties was better than none at all.[38] This argument implied that a rejection of the treaties on the basis of the *Junktim* would allow the Soviet Union to claim that West Germany had prevented détente.

The *Junktim* had firmly linked the conclusion of an acceptable Berlin agreement with the ratification of the Soviet-West German treaty and the Polish-West German treaty. Chancellor Brandt had thus placed the Berlin negotiations in the larger context of the success or failure of West Germany's efforts to improve East-West relations as a whole. If the Berlin talks failed to produce agreement, West Germany's policy of détente would presumably fail also, unless the Federal Republic's treaties with Poland and the Soviet Union were ratified in the absence of an agreement on Berlin. Critics charged that Wehner's suggestion that the *Junktim* could be dissolved showed that the SPD was prepared to renege on its own commitments. The *Junktim* would have value only if there was absolutely no doubt that the West German government would abide by its decision. It was this possibility that West Germany would settle for too little just for the sake of achieving an agreement that Acheson had spoken of in December.

---

[38] Ibid., 8 January 1971.

There was, however, dissension within the SPD on the matter of breaking the *Junktim*. Klaus-Peter Schulz, a member of the Bundestag from West Berlin, pointed out that the *Junktim* had been created by the West German government as a means to ensure the conclusion of an acceptable Berlin agreement because the Soviet government, by its own admission, placed a great deal of value on the ratification of its treaty with West Germany. Schulz, who left the SPD to join the CDU in October 1971, maintained that if the treaties with the Soviet Union and Poland were to represent a contribution to détente, they could not be considered to have a value in themselves (*Selbstwert*).[39] He suggested that the Soviet leaders should not be given the impression, as he believed Wehner had given them, that the Federal Republic was prepared to accept the Soviet position that détente in Berlin was unconnected with the improvement of Soviet-German relations and détente in Europe. Schulz's point was that if the Soviet Union was not prepared to contribute to détente in Berlin, then the value of Soviet assurances that it wished détente with the Federal Republic would be questionable and the value of the Soviet-West German treaty negligible.

The arguments over how best to deal with East Germany and to use the *Junktim* had a certain immediacy in January. During the middle of January traffic was interfered with twice. For the first time in eight years, the Soviet government interfered with Allied military traffic. The day after this interference, the deputy minister-president of the Soviet Union declared during his visit to Düsseldorf that if a solution were found for the "West Berlin problem" such incidents would not occur in the future. That the Soviets would interfere with military traffic raised doubts as to how strongly they objected to East German interference with civilian traffic. In addition some government officials in Bonn speculated that the Soviet Union would not adopt a "more flexible position" until after the Soviet-West German treaty had been discussed at the Twenty-fourth Congress of the Communist Party of the Soviet Union, scheduled for March 1971.

The second traffic interference, with delays lasting up to thirty hours at the border check points, was associated with an FDP meeting in Berlin near the end of the month. Not only did the FDP hold its meeting there but Chancellor Brandt and President Heinemann visited the city the same day. Ambassador Abrasimov had warned the Western

[39] See Theo Sommer, "Spiegelfechtereien um Berlin," *Die Zeit,* 12 January 1971, and *Frankfurter Allgemeine Zeitung,* 6 and 8 January 1971.

ambassadors at the thirteenth quadripartite meeting on 19 January that should federal presence be demonstrated, traffic would be harassed.[40]

On 27 January, a spokesman for the United States government in Berlin declared that it was "the sole responsibility of the three Western Allies to determine which meetings took place in their sectors" and that interference with Berlin traffic would have a "negative effect" on the quadripartite talks. When the harassment continued into February, embassy counselors of France, Great Britain and the United States cancelled the meeting with their Soviet counterpart that was designed to prepare for the fourteenth quadripartite meeting scheduled for 8 February.[41]

Government officials in West Berlin and West Germany were seriously concerned by this round of harassment. Chancellor Brandt and Mayor Schütz both condemned Soviet and East German approval of the harassment.[42] And Mayor Schütz, building the Western case on precedent, stressed that visits of federal officials constituted a part of the "established ties" between West Berlin and West Germany. The only violation that had occurred was the GDR's attempt to interfere in the internal affairs of the city. Two days later he charged that new interference with Berlin traffic represented a return to cold war methods.[43]

Chancellor Brandt reaffirmed the position of his government in his 1971 *Bericht zur Lage der Nation,* delivered to the West German Bundestag on 28 January, and in a speech to the West Berlin *Abgeordnetenhaus* on 30 January. He made special efforts to assure the Soviet government and the Western powers that the Federal Republic would not endorse any position on Berlin that could be interpreted as a concession to Soviet pressure. He emphasized that the *Junktim* remained in effect. While the Federal Republic had been consulting with the Western governments to coordinate their position on Berlin, it did not consider itself to be pressured by time. He said that an acceptable agreement would have to include the principles of *Zugang, Zuordnung,* and *Zutritt,* and that West Germany's Ostpolitik rested on "the promotion of Western European cooperation" and "the further development

---

[40] *Frankfurter Allgemeine Zeitung,* 14 and 22 January and 1 February 1971. See also the *New York Times,* 25 January 1971 and *Der Tagesspiegel,* 13, 15 and 30 January and 4 February 1971.

[41] *Der Tagesspiegel,* 28 and 30 January 1971; *New York Times,* 3 February 1971.

[42] *Neues Deutschland,* 28 January 1971 and Moscow Radio in German broadcast to Germany, 1609 GMT, 27 January 1971.

[43] *Frankfurter Allgemeine Zeitung,* 26 and 28 January 1971.

of the Atlantic Alliance" as well as with the Federal Republic's own efforts to achieve détente.[44]

In Berlin the chancellor referred to these latter points and emphasized that the Western powers agreed on the "criteria and content of a Berlin agreement." It was apparent, he continued, that effective détente (*wirksame Entspannung*) between the Federal Republic and the Soviet Union and for Europe generally would prove impossible if Berlin continued to remain a source of tension (*Spannung*). The chancellor said that it was mandatory that the right of free assembly in West Berlin be maintained and that the Soviet Union had understood the *Junktim* from the beginning. He added that it was important that in the future the "German Democratic Republic did not presume what does and does not constitute a violation of the city's status." [45]

Deputy Press Secretary von Wechmar supported the chancellor's statements. He repeated at the beginning of February that the Soviet Union understood the "indissoluble factual connection" between ratification of the treaty with the Soviet Union and the conclusion of a satisfactory Berlin agreement, and he added that to restrict the right of free assembly would not be in accordance with the mutual recognition of existing realities in Europe. While pressure on access to West Berlin testified to the necessity of an agreement, it was a "useless attempt" to influence the negotiations. He concluded that both unimpeded access and recognition of the city's ties with West Germany were essential for an acceptable agreement.[46]

In an editorial on 3 February, *Neues Deutschland* reasserted the East German position, noting that the German Democratic Republic was "forced" by the FDP meeting to exercise legal countermeasures. The editorial carefully avoided referring to West Berlin as an independent political entity. Instead, it stressed that the countermeasures were not caused by the special situation of West Berlin but by the West German government's attempt to misuse West Berlin. Such a misuse was contrary to East Germany's legitimate interests and to the spirit of the postwar agreements. The editorialist wrote that the FDP meeting was "incompatible with the special situation of West Berlin" and was

---

[44] Deutscher Bundestag, 6. Wahlperiode, 93. Sitzung, 28 January 1971.

[45] Chancellor Brandt's remarks are contained in the *Frankfurter Allgemeine Zeitung*, 1 and 2 February 1971. For the opposite claim see *Neues Deutschland*, 3 February 1971.

[46] *Frankfurter Allgemeine Zeitung*, 2 February 1971.

an attempt to delay détente. He added that the diplomats of several Western countries, including the CDU/CSU bloc, were trying to force the West German government to obtain unilateral concessions from East Germany and the Soviet Union on Berlin.

Joachim Boelke, writing in the 4 February *Der Tagesspiegel,* believed the lack of reference to West Berlin as an independent political entity to be significant. He suggested the editorial was probably written by a Soviet author. Boelke interpreted the article as an accusation that the United States was seeking to inhibit both the progress of Chancellor Brandt's Ostpolitik and the conclusion of an acceptable Berlin agreement. He pointed to the deliberate inference that Chancellor Brandt was not observing previous agreements with the Soviet Union to limit the exercise of demonstrative federal presence. The reference to the special situation in West Berlin implied, according to Boelke, that East Germany, if not the Soviet Union, was prepared to withdraw its claim that West Berlin was an independent political entity in exchange for a reduction in federal presence. Boelke believed that this article represented another attempt to "drive a wedge between the policy of the Federal Republic and the policy of the Western Allies." If it was, it was unsuccessful. The Allies continued to discuss the implications of federal presence without any noticeable policy rift.

Concession and Compromise

The fourteenth and fifteenth quadripartite meetings were held on 8 and 18 February. Between these meetings, for the first time, the West German government and Western officials made explicit how and on what issues they would be prepared to compromise in order to reach an agreement. On 14 February Minister for Intra-German Relations Egon Franke suggested in an interview with the *Frankfurter Allgemeine Zeitung* that while cabinet ministers and other government officials would continue to visit Berlin, it was conceivable that they would not perform official acts (*Amtshandlungen*). He emphasized that federal presence had been exercised because the demonstrations were so effective in asserting the ties between West Berlin and the Federal Republic. If the Soviet Union would recognize the political, financial, and cultural ties between West Berlin and Bonn, the demonstrations would no longer have to be performed. The issue was not demonstrative presence, he pointed out, but whether the living conditions could be

71

improved for West Berlin's citizens. He added that he wished to make it clear that no one in Bonn would at that time consider any modifications in federal presence in view of the "stubborn attitude of East Berlin." [47]

The minister's statement indicated that the West was prepared to compromise on the question of demonstrative federal presence if living conditions could be improved for West Berliners. Presumably the reference to improved living conditions was to be interpreted as meaning a guarantee of *Zugang, Zuordnung* and *Zutritt*. His point, that the purpose of demonstrative presence was to emphasize the city's ties, was well understood in West Berlin and West Germany, and the West German government presumably consulted with the three powers before it publicly presented this possibility of a compromise.

The issue of federal presence was a sensitive one in West Germany. While both the government and the opposition agreed that a Berlin settlement was necessary, the CDU/CSU was by no means in agreement with the government that demonstrative federal presence was the counter to be bargained away. Chancellor Brandt had pointed out in his *Bericht zur Lage der Nation* of January 1970 that officials of the Federal Republic enjoyed the same right to visit West Berlin in an official capacity as did the members of the East German government to visit East Berlin. The government's critics agreed that modifications of federal presence without a Soviet quid pro quo were unacceptable. Indeed many members of the CDU and the CSU believed that no reduction in federal presence was acceptable. Moreover, these critics held that it was the Soviet position and not the East German position that mattered. To announce that a compromise on demonstrative federal presence was possible, they believed, constituted an invitation to the Soviet government to continue its insistence that reduction of such presence was necessary. It could also strengthen the intransigence of the East German government.

Since the official Western position on possible compromises had not yet been released, and since representatives of the CDU/CSU were not privy to all details of the negotiations, the critics of the West German government's policy on Berlin could not substantiate their attacks. Their speculation on demonstrative presence and East German intransigence appeared to be only speculation. Nevertheless members

[47] Ibid., 15 February 1971.

of the CDU/CSU could suspect, and on the basis of previous experience with the Soviet Union and East Germany did suspect, that the East would not agree to an equitable compromise. As a consequence of the lack of public information and in view of the postwar history of Berlin, criticism of Chancellor Brandt's endorsement of détente grew steadily as the new year progressed and as the Berlin negotiations continued without apparent progress.[48]

Several days after the interview with Minister Franke, on 17 and 18 February, the *Frankfurter Allgemeine Zeitung* published a report on a position paper Ambassadors Rush (United States), Sauvagnargues (France), and Jackling (Great Britain) had presented to Ambassador Abrasimov on 8 February. According to the newspaper, the Western powers were willing to compromise on demonstrative presence in exchange for a Soviet guarantee of free and unrestricted access. The Western powers were willing to forego their claim that West Berlin was an integral part of the Federal Republic and would limit demonstration of federal presence, including such official acts as the election of the federal president and meetings of the Bundestag and the cabinet.

A similar report was published in the *New York Times* on 15 February. The *Times* reported that the Western Allies "feel the meetings have reached a stage where the talks can be substantial," and that "on the Western side there has been close consultation with Bonn, and no serious problem is expected in tearing loose the constitutional connection between West Germany and West Berlin." Following the 18 February quadripartite meeting, Chancellor Brandt said in a news conference in Berlin that "the West is aiming at a Berlin settlement that improves the status of the city and insures a stable development." He repeated that for this development to be stable, intra-German talks could proceed only on the basis of a framework worked out by the four powers.[49]

In a move that both the SPD-FDP and the CDU/CSU interpreted as an attempt to change Berlin's status before a quadripartite settlement was reached, Chairman Stoph announced that he was prepared to discuss pass agreements for West Berliners if West Germany halted its illegal political activities. Stoph made this announcement in a meeting with Gerhard Danelius, chairman of the West Berlin Communist party

---

[48] See, for example, ibid., 28 December 1970, and 1, 8 and 12 February 1971.
[49] See the *New York Times,* 20 February 1971.

(SEW). Four days later, on 8 February, Danelius said that he would transmit Chairman Stoph's message to the West Berlin government.[50]

Deputy Press Secretary von Wechmar immediately denounced the proposal as inappropriate because pass agreements involved the problem of access (*Zutritt*), and they were thus in the province of the quadripartite negotiations. Secretary von Wechmar added that it was peculiar for the East German government to issue the announcement through the West Berlin Communist party because at that time the party was participating in the West Berlin elections scheduled for March. He implied that Chairman Stoph was seeking to influence the elections, since West Berliners had not had the opportunity to visit friends in the East since 1966. Presumably, with visits to East Berlin and East Germany as an enticement, the West Berlin population should vote for the Communist party if the Senat refused to negotiate.[51]

Chairman Stoph repeated his offer on 24 February in a letter to Mayor Schütz. Suggesting that the East German government and the West Berlin Senat begin discussions of the visits of West Berlin residents to the East, Stoph explained that the proposal was being made because the GDR placed "great significance on the current efforts for détente in the center of Europe and for the normalization of the situation in West Berlin." If all went well, he suggested, it might be possible to arrange for visits during the Easter holidays. Both Press Secretary Ahlers and Mayor Schütz replied that the proposal exhibited "good will" and that both sides wished the negotiations to be brought to a successful conclusion. As Secretary von Wechmar had pointed out during the first offer, this represented another attempt to persuade the West Berlin government to negotiate unilaterally and thus to act as an independent political entity.[52]

This exchange of letters did initiate discussions on general questions of improving communications between East and West Berlin. *Senatsdirektor* Ulrich Müller represented West Berlin and Günther Kohrt, the state secretary in the East German foreign ministry, repre-

50 *Die Wahrheit,* 4 through 7, and 9 February 1971. *Die Wahrheit* is printed in West Berlin and is the organ of the Socialist Unity party (SEW) in West Berlin.

51 *Frankfurter Allgemeine Zeitung,* 5 February 1971.

52 A copy of Chairman Stoph's letter is printed in ibid., 26 February 1971, and the mayor's letter is reprinted in ibid., 27 February 1971. See also David Binder, "German Reds Ease Position on Berlin," *New York Times,* 26 February 1971; the editorial "Stoph's Osterei" in the 26 February *Frankfurter Allgemeine Zeitung;* and Joachim Boelke, "Die Antwort," *Der Tagesspiegel,* 27 February 1971.

sented East Berlin. But when Müller refused to discuss specific issues of access for West Berliners to East Berlin without prior four-power authorization, the East Germans refused to grant the holiday visits. It would seem to be unrealistic to assume that East Germany really thought it could boost the West Berlin Communist party's share of the vote in the upcoming elections with the issue of the pass agreements. In the 15 March elections, the Communist party in West Berlin received 2.3 percent of the total votes cast.[53]

---

[53] *Der Tagesspiegel,* 16 March 1971. See also Joachim Boelke, "Endlich Vertagt," ibid., 13 May 1971.

4

The Negotiations: Conclusion

The first year of negotiations produced no tangible improvements in living conditions for the West Berliners. And after that year, the issues were not any more clearly drawn than they had been before. There had been one report suggesting what the West was willing to consider as possible compromises. There had been several unofficial reports that West German officials were willing to consider a reduction of demonstrative federal presence in West Berlin. The absence of discussion on specific concessions and possible compromises suggested that the negotiations had a long way to go before an agreement could be signed.

March 1971

March began with harassment on the autobahns during a meeting of the CDU/CSU leaders in West Berlin. Mayor Schütz again declared this interference demonstrated the importance of the city's ties with the Federal Republic and the need for an agreement on Berlin. On the same day, the *Frankfurter Allgemeine Zeitung* published reports that officials in Washington considered prospects for a Berlin settlement to be "disappointingly small" and that Western officials had postponed the next quadripartite meeting.[1]

In an interview on the West German radio, *Südwestfunk*, Chancellor Brandt said it was improbable that the negotiations would fail. He reviewed the requirements for *Zugang, Zuordnung,* and *Zutritt.* He carefully defined West Berlin's ties with the Federal Republic. He spoke

---

[1] *Frankfurter Allgemeine Zeitung,* 4 March 1971.

of an administrative interweaving (*administrative Verzahnung*) in which federal presence would be included and which would permit the Bundestag or its representatives to visit the city on official matters pertaining to West Berlin and added that during the continuing negotiations the Western powers would welcome a certain reserve in the demonstration of federal presence. The chancellor was not entirely specific on what demonstrative federal presence included, and former Foreign Minister Gerhard Schröder (a member of the CDU) criticized him for differentiating between the "normal" and the "demonstrative" aspects of federal presence in West Berlin.[2]

On 12 March, a day after Foreign Minister Scheel had taken issue with reports from Washington and claimed that the talks were indeed progressing, the *Frankfurter Allgemeine Zeitung* listed the issues being discussed by the four powers. The first issue was the dispute over methods to empower the German Democratic Republic and the Federal Republic to discuss the details of unrestricted traffic. This was a question of East German sovereignty. In claiming to be a sovereign state East Germany could not permit another country, the Soviet Union, to be ultimately responsible for handling traffic details within its borders. The second issue was the dispute over representation of West Berlin abroad. West Berlin's political status hinged on this question. The Soviet Union wanted Great Britain, France, and the United States to handle all diplomatic details for the city. It had reportedly relaxed its position and was willing to let West Germany negotiate trade agreements for West Berlin. In addition there was discussion on the question of diplomatic representation for the Soviet Union in West Berlin and on the dispute over federal presence.

A week later Valentin Falin, later to be the Soviet ambassador to West Germany, met with Jürgen Echternach, chairman of the CDU organization *Junge Union*. Falin repeated the claim that West Berlin was an independent political entity. He spoke of the Allied suspension of Articles 23 and 144 (2) of the West German Basic Law in 1949 and asserted that not only was West Berlin not a West German state (Land) and not a constituent part of West Germany, but also that federal presence in West Berlin was illegal. He argued, moreover, that if the Federal Republic considered its presence in West Berlin to be a postwar fact, so did the German Democratic Republic and the Soviet

---

[2] Ibid., 8 March 1971. See also Joachim Boelke's editorials "Heute wieder mit Abrassimow" and "Wenig Überraschungen," *Der Tagesspiegel,* 9 and 12 March 1971.

Union consider their protests—that is, harassment—to be part of the status quo. On the other hand he said that the four powers were discussing West German diplomatic representation of West Berlin in an effort to find a solution for the problem, and he endorsed a Berlin agreement that would respect the rights of the West Berliners and the German Democratic Republic, adding that East Germany could give guarantees of free and unrestricted access so long as its rights were not affected.[3]

His remarks were interpreted by the liberal West German daily *Frankfurter Rundschau* as indicating what had in fact been known for a long time—that a satisfactory solution for Berlin traffic, for greater freedom of movement for West Berliners, and for recognition of the economic, cultural and legal ties with West Germany would only be possible in return for a reduction in the demonstration of federal presence and acknowledgment that West Berlin was not a Land. The newspaper continued that demonstrations of West Berlin's ties with the Federal Republic would be superfluous if the Soviet Union recognized the principle of the legal, cultural, and economic ties in the quadripartite agreement.[4]

Ambassador Abrasimov submitted a corroborative position paper to the Western ambassadors on 25 March. Press Secretary Ahlers also acknowledged that Ambassador Falin's analysis was an accurate description of the Soviet government's negotiating position. He emphasized that only the form of federal presence was being discussed, federal presence itself being indispensable to an acceptable Berlin agreement. Von Wechmar expanded Ahler's remarks in a press conference the next day. He said that a Berlin agreement would not be possible without Soviet recognition of West Berlin's ties with the Federal Republic. If these ties with the Federal Republic were assured, continued demonstrations of federal presence would no longer be necessary. In keeping with this exchange, Foreign Minister Scheel referred to the demonstration of federal presence in West Berlin as "abnormal," adding that the Federal Republic had been able to develop its ties with Berlin only by permission of the three Western powers.[5]

---

[3] See the *Frankfurter Allgemeine Zeitung,* 19, 20 and 30 March 1971, particularly the article by Nikolas Benckiser, "Falin deckt die Karten auf," in the 20 March issue.

[4] *Frankfurter Rundschau,* 20 and 21 March 1971; *Frankfurter Allgemeine Zeitung,* 22 March 1971.

[5] *Frankfurter Allgemeine Zeitung,* 22 and 23 March 1971.

The CDU/CSU did not approve of the implications of these remarks. They believed that West Germany was conceding far more on West Berlin than was necessary. If both sides were supposed to recognize existing conditions in Berlin, then West Germany had the same right in West Berlin as East Germany had in East Berlin, consistent with Chancellor Brandt's conclusion in his *Bericht zur Lage der Nation* of January 1970.

These exchanges represented a significant change, not because negotiating positions had altered (they had not) but because disputed topics were being increasingly discussed in public. In addition there was an anonymous report from Washington that two working papers were now in existence. The *Frankfurter Allgemeine Zeitung* evaluated the negotiating positions on 31 March:

(1) *Zugang.* The Western Allies maintained that the transportation of persons and goods between West Berlin and West Germany should proceed without hindrance with controls limited to the checking of identification papers. The Soviet Union maintained that complete responsibility for this subject rested with the German Democratic Republic whose sovereignty in this area should be recognized by Western powers.

(2) *Zutritt.* The Western Allies wanted the four powers to direct the West Berlin Senat and the German Democratic Republic to conclude agreements to permit West Berliners to visit East Berlin and East Germany on the same basis as citizens of the Federal Republic. The Soviet Union claimed that there was neither cause nor legal basis for such a directive: the four powers could only approve agreements made between the independent political entity of West Berlin and the German Democratic Republic.

(3) *Zuordnung.* The Western Allies were not prepared to recognize any change in federal presence in West Berlin. The Soviet Union wanted the exercise of federal presence and other "provocatory" acts of official West German representatives in West Berlin to cease. The Soviet government also demanded the dissolution of the *Nationalpartei Deutschlands* (NPD)—a neo-nazi party—in West Berlin and the closure of RIAS (*Radio im amerikanischen Sektor*).

(4) *Vertretung,* or, representation. (This issue had existed in the background even before the first proposals for negotiations had been exchanged. It had been overshadowed by *Zugang, Zuordnung,* and *Zutritt,* but now it was beginning to rise to the surface.) The three

Western powers maintained that the diplomatic representation of West Berlin and its population belonged within the province of the Federal Republic. The Soviet Union held West Berlin to be an independent political entity which therefore could not be represented abroad by the Federal Republic.

As Chancellor Brandt confirmed on 1 April, the positions were not very close. Later that day Press Secretary Ahlers noted that the Soviet Union had indicated that the negotiations would not be concluded soon.[6] Secretary Brezhnev, however, in remarks to the Twenty-fourth Congress of the Communist Party of the Soviet Union declared that if the Western powers would proceed "from respect for the allied agreements which determine the special status of West Berlin and respect for the sovereign rights of the GDR as an independent socialist state," there could be a settlement of the problems connected with West Berlin.[7]

The West German government, according to Deputy Press Secretary von Wechmar, believed that Secretary Brezhnev's speech confirmed Soviet willingness to achieve a modus vivendi for European problems,[8] West German officials reaffirmed that the Soviet Union had an interest in achieving détente, and that the Soviets understood the *Junktim*.[9] The unanswered question was how the Soviet Union interpreted détente.

April 1971

An assessment of developments since January suggested that an agreement was still not in the immediate offing. East Germany's harsh policy toward West Berlin continued. Between 14 August 1970 and 31 March 1971 autobahn traffic was interfered with on at least ten occasions— for a total of twenty-five days of harassment and up to thirty hours of delay at the East German border checkpoints. In this same period refugees were fired upon at the Berlin Wall on twenty-one occasions. Of the rounds fired, 375 caused personal injury or material damage in West Berlin. Between January and April 1971 the East Germans

---

[6] Ibid., 2 April 1971.

[7] "Report of the CPSU Central Committee to the 24th Congress of the Communist Party of the Soviet Union," delivered by Leonid Brezhnev, 30 March 1971 (Moscow: Novosti Press Agency Publishing House, 1971), pp. 43-44.

[8] *Relay from Bonn,* 14 April 1971.

[9] *Frankfurter Allgemeine Zeitung,* 23 April 1971.

had arrested 134 persons, detained 108 persons for questioning, and denied 240 persons permission to use the autobahns.[10]

The growing length of the negotiations was also a problem for the West. On 13 April Deputy Press Secretary von Wechmar accused the East German government of being primarily responsible for the "present difficulties on the path to détente." [11] Since the East German government was concerned that the Soviet Union might compromise its claim to sovereignty over access to West Berlin, harassment did seem to be the logical tool to use to force recognition of East Germany's sovereignty. But it was also clear that the Soviet Union was interested in aiding the East Germans to establish sovereignty as Soviet officials had repeatedly stated since the beginning of the year. They had supported East German objections to Western actions. Ambassador Abrasimov had indicated Soviet support for the East German objection to the demonstration of federal presence in West Berlin. And future Ambassador Falin had indicated three weeks earlier that the continued demonstration of federal presence would preclude a Berlin agreement.

The CDU and the CSU, in criticizing Willy Brandt, stressed that there was little difference between the basic foreign policy of East Germany and that of the Soviet Union. They reasoned that East Germany's interference with access was inconceivable without Soviet support. Joachim Boelke agreed that the foreign policies of the GDR and the Soviet Union were not very different. According to Boelke, it simply did not make sense to imply that the Soviet Union was a "secret ally of Bonn against Ulbricht." [12] Discussions of blame, however, like rationalization, did nothing to break the impasse.

In violation of an agreement among the four ambassadors to keep the Berlin negotiations confidential, the Soviet Union leaked its working paper for the 26 March meeting to a Polish newspaper, *Zycie Warszawy,* which carried it as an article on 15 April, a day before the eighteenth quadripartite meeting. It was reprinted in *Neues Deutschland* and distributed by Tass the next day.

The article in *Zycie Warszawy,* attributed to anonymous sources in Brussels, emphasized "humanitarian aspects" which were supposed to indicate Soviet willingness to compromise. The Soviet government

---

[10] West Berlin officials kindly provided this information in answer to a letter from the author.

[11] *Der Tagesspiegel,* 14 April 1971.

[12] Joachim Boelke, "Zwei östliche Publikationen," *Der Tagesspiegel,* 16 April 1971.

declared its willingness (1) to recognize the existing ties between West Berlin and West Germany, (2) to accept West Berlin's diplomatic representation by Bonn, (3) to recognize treaties permitting West Berliners to travel to East Germany and East Berlin for personal, cultural, religious or humanitarian reasons, or as tourists, (4) to permit traffic to proceed without impediment on the basis of generally accepted norms, and (5) to permit West Berlin's inclusion in all treaties concluded by the Federal Republic as long as the treaty partners are in agreement and the treaty is not of a political or military nature.[13]

The publication of the Soviet working paper was received with reserve in Western capitals. Von Wechmar explained on 16 April that the paper had been published in incomplete form and thus presented an overly favorable picture of the Soviet position. The purpose of the publication had been to lend credence to Soviet assurances of a desire to compromise without drawing attention to the different options the Soviet Union would still have with respect to interpreting the document's political significance for the status of West Berlin. At the end of April, the Soviet paper, along with the Western position paper of 5 February, was published in several West German dailies including the *Generalanzeiger* (Bonn), *Der Tagesspiegel* (Berlin), and the *Hannoversche Allgemeine Zeitung*.[14]

A close analysis of the Soviet position paper showed that Moscow sought Western agreement to a change in West Berlin's status. The paper referred to "the interests" of the Soviet Union in West Berlin without specifying what those interests were. It proposed the establishment of consular offices to deal with economic and property matters in the city. It acknowledged that existing quadripartite agreements pertaining to existing conditions should remain valid, but it did not define these conditions. Instead it referred to the "existing situation" in the area under negotiation without defining the area or the situation. The paper did say that the situation in the area could not be unilaterally changed. The *Frankfurter Allgemeine Zeitung* (16 April) concluded that this represented a Soviet attempt to determine what would and would not be permitted in West Berlin in the future. The Soviet paper went on to propose that, according to the principles of international

---

[13] *Frankfurter Allgemeine Zeitung,* 16 April 1971; *Der Tagesspiegel,* 16 April 1971.

[14] In late July Axel Springer, a noted conservative, published the Soviet position paper in *Quick* directing to Chancellor Brandt the question "How long do you wish to dance to Moscow's pipe?"

law, all acts constituting interference in the internal affairs of third parties which endangered public order and security should be avoided in the future. These acts were not defined.

The paper also said that since West Berlin was not a constituent part of the Federal Republic, its citizens could not possess West German citizenship. The interests of the West German government in relation to the West Berlin Senat and the three Western powers should be represented by a special federal representative who would establish his office in West Berlin. In addition, meetings and official acts of the federal president, of the Bundesversammlung, the Bundestag, and the Bundesrat, or of their parties or blocs, as well as of other federal institutions should be eliminated if they represented an extension of official competence to West Berlin.

The references to traffic were more detailed and foresaw the transportation of goods in sealed vehicles through the German Democratic Republic upon inspection of papers at the border. In the future the tolls for use of the autobahns were to be paid in a flat amount by the West German government instead of individual payment, so as to contribute to the flow of traffic. The Soviet position paper insisted that the details of the transit agreements be concluded by the East and West German governments. Their accords would then become part of the quadripartite agreement. The procedure for empowering the German Democratic Republic to conclude the agreement was circuitous. Intra-German negotiations would start after the three Western powers received a Soviet declaration based on a statement by the East German government that it was willing to discuss the issue of access with the participating parties. This same procedure was to be used to empower discussion on the arrangements for West Berliners to visit East Berlin and East Germany. This procedure emphasized East German sovereignty.

Press Secretary Ahlers said that the Soviet paper did contain positive elements for discussion, although negotiating positions remained far apart. Official West German statements were being phrased in such a way as to suggest that a distinction was being made between the political and the practical aspects of the Berlin problem. Chancellor Brandt and Press Secretary Ahlers both stated in late April that agreements could be made on practical issues with the Soviet Union.[15] The inherent problem with such an attempt, if it was to be more than an

---

[15] *Der Tagesspiegel,* 20, 23 and 24 April 1971.

analytical tool, was that *Zugang, Zuordnung,* and *Zutritt* were just as much political problems as they were practical problems. More precisely, they were the practical aspects of basic political differences. For example, *Zuordnung* was a practical problem because businesses needed some assurance of continued financial connections with West Germany, but it is difficult to imagine how the practical matter of financial and legal ties could be solved without West Berlin's political ties with West Germany being settled first. Furthermore, the Soviet Union could argue in the future that the solution of a practical problem, if such was achieved, inherently altered the political status of the city. Since it was highly unlikely that a perfect agreement would be reached, it would be wise to make sure that short-term benefits would not become long-term disasters.

Demonstration of Federal Presence

By the middle of April there was no longer much doubt that the demonstrative federal presence would be reduced and that this was the practical side of a political issue of major importance in the negotiations. The full significance of this did not become evident until May. The FDP monthly *Liberal* published an article entitled *"Schwierigkeiten einer Berlinregelung"* (Difficulties of a Berlin Settlement) by "Wieland Deutsch." The article was controversial not merely because it discussed the legality of West Berlin's ties with West Germany, but also because the authors using the pseudonym were supposed to be Deputy Press Secretary Rüdiger von Wechmar and Günther van Well, the deputy director of the political section of the West German foreign office.[16]

The article was written for a specific reason. It was an attempt to explain to the general public that federal presence was going to be reduced, why it was necessary for federal presence to be reduced, and why this would not affect the city's status. The article argued that by continuing to observe the quadripartite status of the city, the Western powers would retain their legal rights of occupation. While the West German Constitutional Court (*Bundesverfassungsgericht*) had ruled as recently as the 1966 Niekisch case that West Berlin was a Land of the Federal Republic, the article pointed out that the relevant parts of the West German Basic Law, Articles 23 and 144 (2), had been suspended

---

[16] Ibid., 9 June 1971. The article by "Wieland Deutsch" that appeared in the May issue of *Liberal* was reprinted in *Der Tagesspiegel,* 10 June 1971.

85

by the Allies. Thus, the authors argued, there was no legal basis from which the West German government could demonstrate federal presence in West Berlin. One could not expect the Soviet Union to conclude a Berlin agreement which permitted the continued demonstration of the federal presence. "Wieland Deutsch" concluded that should the demonstration of federal presence be reduced, the Soviet Union was prepared to make concessions. He maintained that the West could not negotiate simply on alleged legal positions (*vermeintliche Rechtspositionen*) but must deal with the practical matters of access, the city's ties with West Germany, and the security of the free and democratic order of Berlin. This approach was the only alternative open to the West at this time. It might have been possible once to argue that the German Democratic Republic had no legal right to establish its capital in the Soviet sector, but in 1971 this was no longer possible. The West had accepted de facto the transformation of the Soviet sector into the capital city of the German Democratic Republic.[17]

The resulting arguments over the legal status of West Berlin were the subject of debate in West Germany until the signing of the Berlin agreement.[18] The CDU and the CSU seized upon the point as an opportunity to criticize the chancellor's Ostpolitik. The CDU/CSU argued that just as the Soviet sector had been incorporated into the German Democratic Republic by Soviet desire, so federal presence in West Berlin had been demonstrated with the permission of the Western powers since 1949. The one was just as much an accepted fact as the other. To renounce the demonstration of federal presence unilaterally was inconsistent with mutual recognition of European realities as they had developed since 1949. If the Western powers were prepared to acknowledge the Soviet sector as the capital of the German

---

[17] The relevant documents that deal with the suspension are contained in *Dokumente zur Berlin-Frage 1944-1966,* pp. 114-120. Detlef Merten of the Free University of Berlin has written a succinct analysis of the legal relationship between West Berlin and West Germany, "Zur Rechtslage Berlins," in *Berlin als unternehmerische Aufgabe* (Wiesbaden: Betriebswirtschaftlicher Verlag Dr. Th. Gabler, 1971), pp. 71-125. Abercrombie Fitzwiggen of London also provided me with useful information on this matter.

[18] See Rolf Zundel, "Wieland Deutsch oder Boris Russ?" *Die Zeit,* 22 June 1971; Erich Roper, "Zur Rechtslage Berlins," *Deutschland Archiv,* no. 8 (August 1971), pp. 801-804; Hans-Heinrich Mahncke, "Zur Rechtslage Berlins: Einige korrigierende Bemerkungen," ibid., no. 9 (September 1971), pp. 901-909, and "Noch einmal: Zur Rechtslage Berlins," ibid., no. 11 (November 1971), pp. 1132-1136. See also Jens Hacker, "Der neue Rechtsstatus für West-Berlin," *Die Politische Meinung,* no. 142 (1972), pp. 78-94.

Democratic Republic, then the Soviet Union should be forced to recognize West Berlin as a part of the Federal Republic of Germany without demanding any reduction in federal presence. This argument was not without logic, but East Germany and the Soviet Union enjoyed the control of access to Berlin and that was a major trump.

The End of Deadlock: May–September 1971

Egon Bahr announced on 20 May that the structure of a Berlin agreement was settled. He added that this structure would also be used for treaties between East and West Germany and between the West Berlin Senat and East Germany.[19] It was unclear, however, what had happened to break the deadlock.

On 21 May Bahr met with Secretary Kohl in East Berlin. In a statement issued after the meeting he suggested that while no change was expected in the East German position, a new phase was beginning. Erich Honecker had replaced Walter Ulbricht as first secretary of the East German Communist party (SED). Ulbricht had been ill for over a year and had resigned at the beginning of May. Whether or not Honecker's succession as secretary was the turning point in the negotiations is debatable. The transition was smooth and Ulbricht was accorded the honorary position of chairman of the SED, a post created especially for him. But it did seem that East Germany was modifying its hard stance toward the negotiations. Two weeks after Honecker assumed office he traveled to Moscow with Willi Stoph. In a communiqué issued following their meeting with Secretary Brezhnev, they agreed "that an understanding on the question of Berlin would meet the interests of all parties to the negotiations and would remove the grounds for disputes and conflicts in this region." [20]

Reports circulated in Washington that the Soviet Union could be expected to modify its position on Berlin. These reports took into account the Soviet-American decision to break the impasse in the SALT talks by limiting discussion to antimissile defenses, and by Secretary Brezhnev's announcement in Tiflis on 14 May that his government wished to begin exploratory talks with the United States on troop

[19] *Frankfurter Allgemeine Zeitung,* 20 and 22 May 1971.

[20] Chalmers Roberts, "Soviet Move on Berlin Impasse Is Expected," *Washington Post,* 25 May 1971. See also Ernst-Ulrich Fromm, "Moskau baut seine deutschen Gefolgsleute aus Ostberlin auf," *Die Welt,* 12 July 1971. Walter Ulbricht died on 1 August 1973 in East Berlin; he was eighty years old.

reductions in Europe. Despite a West German official's opinion published in the 27 May *New York Times* "that the Russians intend to carry these negotiations to the point where agreement is almost but not quite within reach . . . [and] bring the strategic-arms limitation talks or perhaps the troop-cut idea into play as a means of pressuring the West for last-minute concessions on Berlin," a Defense Department spokesman was quoted in the same article as "feeling . . . that the talks on troop cuts will be at least as difficult as those on strategic arms already have been—so that a Berlin settlement will precede agreement on troop cuts, if there is to be a Berlin settlement at all."

At the beginning of June, Chancellor Brandt warned that improvements could only be expected on procedural issues related to practical questions because positions on the political questions were still so far apart.[21] Echoing the same theme, Herbert Wehner predicted that a Berlin agreement would be reached even though it might not satisfy everyone.[22] The *Frankfurter Allgemeine Zeitung* criticized Wehner in a 7 June editorial for "the willingness to give up as much of his own position as necessary for agreement." But the West German government qualified its position. That same day Press Secretary Ahlers endorsed the NATO ministers' decision to make an acceptable Berlin agreement a prerequisite for multilateral preparations for a conference on security and cooperation in Europe. On 7 June, Soviet Ambassador Abrasimov was quoted in the West German press as saying that if it were dependent on the Soviet Union, an agreement would be concluded before the end of the year.[23] The following day, the *New York Times* reported that a tentative consensus had been reached by the four powers on the issue of access. That Chancellor Brandt held it to be possible to separate political from practical matters in the Berlin problem did not mean, however, that either East Germany or the Soviet Union was prepared to accept the separation. Nikolai Podgorny, president of the Supreme Soviet, declared in Moscow on 11 June that the Soviet government hoped it would be possible to remove the artificial impediments blocking a mutually acceptable agreement. But his insertion of the phrase "a mutually acceptable agreement for West Berlin" indicated a political interpretation unacceptable to the West.[24]

---

[21] *Die Presse* (Vienna), 1 June 1971.
[22] *Frankfurter Allgemeine Zeitung,* 4 through 7 June 1971.
[23] Ibid., 5 and 8 June 1971.
[24] Ibid., 12 June 1971.

Several days later Erich Honecker delivered his maiden speech to the Eighth Congress of the SED. In his address he referred to West Berlin as a city with a special political status, avoiding the term "independent political entity." The phrase "special political status" had first appeared in a 3 February *Neues Deutschland* editorial and the Western powers had considered it to represent a significant moderation on the part of East Germany. Honecker did not demand the recognition of the German Democratic Republic as a sovereign state before the conclusion of a Berlin agreement, but he did demand that the Federal Republic recognize that West Berlin never had been a part of West Germany and that it had a special political status. "On this basis," he said, "it will be possible to settle all outstanding questions, in the interests of European peace and of the people of West Berlin." [25]

A writer for *Der Spiegel* was not impressed and wrote in the 21 June issue that "thus far solely the GDR had disturbed the harmony." But the West German government was encouraged, especially by Secretary Brezhnev's address to the Eighth Congress of the SED. Secretary Brezhnev did refer to political issues in his speech when he endorsed a rapid conclusion of the four-power discussions on "West Berlin" and when he mentioned that Berlin had become the capital city of East Germany. But he said that, with "appropriate consideration of the legitimate interests and sovereign rights" of the German Democratic Republic, "we, for our part, are prepared to make efforts to bring this matter to a successful completion and to insure that the agreement reached be effective and carried into life." [26] Chancellor Brandt, discussing the secretary's remarks, attached special importance to the fact that Secretary Brezhnev had gone to East Berlin to deliver his remarks supporting a Berlin settlement. The chancellor believed Brezhnev's speech "made clear the importance which the Soviet Union continues to attach to the treaty signed by the two governments last August in Moscow." [27]

The CDU/CSU now suggested that the Western definition of an acceptable Berlin settlement was gradually being reduced to a "mini-solution." Joachim Nawrocki, writing for *Die Zeit*, argued that while the four powers would never be able to agree on the political status of

[25] *New York Times*, 16 June 1971; Erich Honecker, writing in *Neues Deutschland*, 16 June 1971.

[26] *Neues Deutschland*, 17 June 1971; *New York Times*, 18 June 1971.

[27] *Frankfurter Allgemeine Zeitung*, 18 June 1971; *Relay from Bonn*, 18 June 1971.

Berlin, they would be unable to change it for better or worse.[28] The CDU/CSU were not at all sure that the negotiations should be continued at all under the circumstances. This debate carried through July while the issue of a Soviet consulate general for West Berlin was discussed.

The Soviet Union wished to establish a consulate general in West Berlin as part of an agreement on Berlin. Why the Soviet Union wished to establish such an office and how it would affect the city's status were questions of importance. The Western powers were concerned that a Soviet representative in West Berlin as well as in East Berlin would tend to validate the assertion that only West Berlin was a four-power city, especially since the Western powers were not represented at all in East Berlin. West Berlin's minister of the interior, Kurt Neubauer, believed that this was a possibility and conjectured that the Soviet Union would make that assertion in the future. He regarded the establishment of a consulate general in West Berlin as the transitional stage on the path to political independence for the city. On the other hand, Mayor Schütz suggested that the consulate general would emphasize Soviet recognition of West Berlin's ties with West Germany.[29]

On 18 July *Welt am Sonntag*, a conservative paper sympathetic to the CDU/CSU, published reports of several confidential telegrams the West German ambassador to the United States, Rolf Pauls, had sent to the chancellor's office in April 1971. Later that month *Quick* published similar reports along with partial texts of the telegrams leaked by a West German government official presumably critical of Ostpolitik. According to both reports, Secretary Bahr and West German Ambassador Pauls had met in Washington on 23 April 1971 with Special Advisor on National Security Affairs Henry Kissinger, Undersecretary of State John Irwin, Director of the Office of German Affairs in the State Department James Sutterlin, and Special Advisor to the President Helmut Sonnenfeld. At that meeting, according to the articles, Secretary Bahr suggested that the Western powers could accept the establishment of a Soviet consulate general in West Berlin. He argued that its presence would demonstrate clearly that the Soviet government did not

---

[28] Joachim Nawrocki, "Ein Schritt vorwärts in Berlin," *Die Zeit,* 15 June 1971.

[29] See the remarks of Kurt Neubauer in the SPD weekly, *Berliner Stimme,* early July 1971. These were reprinted in *Frankfurter Allgemeine Zeitung,* 7 July 1971. Mayor Schütz's comments are in the 1 July issue of the *Frankfurter Allgemeine Zeitung.*

possess original rights in West Berlin. The consulate general, he believed, would signify that the Soviet Union was a foreign power among others having military missions or consulates general in West Berlin accredited to the three Western powers. This accreditation to the Western powers would signify that they were the sole sovereign powers in West Berlin. Bahr believed that Soviet attempts to establish special relations with the West Berlin government would not be inconsistent with relations between the Senat and other missions in West Berlin. According to the reports in *Quick*, he was less specific about the possibility that the Soviet government would later construe this move as proof of West Berlin's independent political status. But he did emphasize that it would be easier to control Soviet activity in West Berlin if there was a consulate general with clear restrictions on its responsibilities and privileges.[30]

The Western Allies, in particular the United States, were less certain that the establishment of a Soviet consulate general in West Berlin would be benign. They pointed out that it would be peculiar if West German federal presence was reduced in West Berlin while that of the Soviet Union was increased.[31] In response to an inquiry whether the consulate general would represent a step toward establishing West Berlin's political independence, Bahr reportedly replied that West Berlin was not a Land, rather it was a "third phenomenon" enjoying a special status. Secretary Bahr justified his proposal on the basis that one must make compromises in order to achieve agreement.[32] The United States was not convinced that the consulate general would not support future Soviet assertions of West Berlin's political independence, especially since East Berlin had become the capital of East Germany. Because the United States government was concerned with this problem, it was the last of the Allies to agree to the establishment of the consulate general. In this connection one State Department official reportedly declared that the United States could not appear to be "more German than the Germans." [33]

---

30 *Quick*, 29 July 1971; *Welt am Sonntag*, 18 July 1971; *Frankfurter Allgemeine Zeitung*, 19 and 24 July 1971.

31 *Welt am Sonntag*, 18 July 1971.

32 *Quick*, 29 July 1971; *Relay from Bonn*, 28 July 1971; *Frankfurter Allgemeine Zeitung*, 19 July 1971. See also Joachim Boelke, "Die Verhandlungskunst," *Der Tagesspiegel*, 21 July 1971.

33 Robert Kleiman, "West Optimistic on Berlin Accord with Soviet Union," and Benjamin Welles, "U.S. Faces Growing Isolation on Berlin," both in the *New*

The CDU/CSU, strongly opposed to the establishment of the consulate general, suggested that Secretary Bahr was exerting pressure on the Western powers to approve an unacceptable compromise. Deputy Press Secretary von Wechmar denied that this was the case.[34] The government's critics questioned the reasoning behind the proposal. Was not Secretary Bahr removing West Berlin from the protection of the 1944 and 1945 four-power agreements by referring to a special status for West Berlin? The CDU/CSU and some members of the SPD agreed with the United States that the consulate general would provide a precedent for future Soviet assertions that West Berlin was in fact an independent political entity.

Secretary Bahr noted that the Soviet government would have established the consulate general in its own right if it had not considered permission necessary.[35] The *Stuttgarter Zeitung,* which supported Ostpolitik, pointed out "that the establishment of a consulate general in West Berlin underscores more than any other kind of representation the fact that the Soviet Union possesses *no* original rights in West Berlin." [36] In addition, Secretary Bahr argued that "should the Federal Republic attain the right to represent West Berlin for instance in Moscow, such a concession would follow a certain logic." [37]

It was clear from discussions in the press that the negotiations had entered a serious stage. For the first time in the negotiations, the four ambassadors met four times in one month. The twenty-third to twenty-sixth sessions were held on 8, 16, 22, and 30 July. On 4 August Rüdiger von Wechmar confirmed that the negotiations were indeed at an important point. He announced in Bonn that, "in the interests of positive progress in the Berlin negotiations, the three Western powers and the Federal government have agreed to maintain strict secrecy and to make no statements in the coming weeks." [38] Five more meetings were held between 11 and 18 August. Following the thirty-third meet-

York Times, 2 August 1971. See also "Nixon Broke W. Berlin Deadlock," *Dallas Morning News,* 31 August 1971.

[34] *Relay from Bonn,* 29 July 1971. See also Joachim Boelke, "Nicht nahtlos," *Der Tagesspiegel,* 13 June 1971.

[35] *Relay from Bonn,* 27 July 1971.

[36] *Stuttgarter Zeitung,* 31 July 1971.

[37] *Relay from Bonn,* 27 July 1971. At the time of the negotiations, West Berliners obtained Soviet visas from the Soviet Intourist travel bureau in the British sector. West German citizens obtained Soviet visas at the Soviet embassy in East Berlin.

[38] Ibid., 5 August 1971.

ing on 23 August, the four powers announced completion of a draft treaty. The four ambassadors signed the agreement on 3 September 1971.

The document signed by the four powers on 3 September was not the complete agreement. It called for the East and West German governments to conclude the necessary accords on the movement of traffic. It also called for the two German governments to work out details on travel, communications, and exchange of territories between East and West Berlin.[39] The transit agreement was concluded on 17 December 1971, and the accord on Berlin was concluded on 20 December 1971. Both accords were then inserted in the 3 September agreement as stipulated. The entire agreement was enacted on 3 June 1972, when the four foreign ministers signed the Final Quadripartite Protocol already contained in the 3 September agreement.

---

[39] The reference to an "exchange of territory" concerns the enclaves belonging to West Berlin that are located within the German Democratic Republic. With some exceptions, these enclaves are not connected to the Western sectors by access roads that belong to West Berlin. An exchange of territory involving West Berlin-East German border adjustments was concluded between West Berlin and East German officials on 20 December 1971. This affects primarily the inhabitants of the enclave Steinstücken. For additional information concerning the origin and legal status of the enclaves, consult the documents and papers in the archives of the *Landesarchiv Berlin*. See also H. M. Catudal, Jr., *Steinstücken: A Study in Cold War Politics* (New York: Vantage Press, 1971).

5
The Agreement

With the official signing of the Berlin agreement on 3 June 1972, the problems of access, communications, travel, and ties with West Germany were reduced in complexity and, in some cases, appear to have been partly resolved. There was no Berlin crisis in 1972. On the contrary, for the first time since 1949 the four powers agreed on many major issues.

Secretary of State William Rogers welcomed the agreement as opening the way for Berlin "to become the hope for the future of Europe" after being for a quarter century the "symbol of division." Foreign Minister Andrei Gromyko viewed it as providing the perspective for "a peaceful and happy future." [1] Erich Honecker welcomed the Berlin accord and the Bundestag's ratification of the Polish and the Soviet treaties as "the beginning of a new phase in the development of European politics and cooperation." Chancellor Brandt said that the Berlin agreement and the Polish and the Russian treaties "will probably . . . be considered a political turning point" in the history of East-West relations. [2]

The full text of the Quadripartite Agreement is printed in the Appendix. Readers will find it helpful to review the agreement both before and after reading this chapter.

[1] The speeches delivered in Berlin on 3 June 1972 by the foreign ministers of France, Great Britain, the Soviet Union, and the United States following the signing of the final protocol to the quadripartite agreement are reprinted in *Der Tagesspiegel*, 4 June 1972.

[2] Erich Honecker's remarks were distributed by the East German news service Allgemeiner Deutscher Nachrichtendienst (ADN) on 5 June 1972. Chancellor Brandt's comments appeared in an interview with *Neue Rheinzeitung*, 6 June 1972.

Reaction to Ostpolitik in West Germany and West Berlin

The reaction of the citizens of West Berlin and of West Germany to Ostpolitik and the Berlin agreement was noteworthy. Their approval of the agreement is best indicated by data derived from public opinion polls. For example, in West Berlin in April of 1972 (eight months after the conclusion of the agreement), 65 percent of the population considered the agreement to be "satisfactory" or "very satisfactory." Five percent expressed no opinion, and 30 percent considered the agreement to be "unsatisfactory." In addition, approximately 85 percent of persons traveling between West Berlin and West Germany, and between West Berlin, East Berlin and the GDR, in April 1972 judged the customs and transit controls at the borders to be "satisfactory." At the same time, 60 percent of West Berlin's population recommended ratification by the Bundestag of West Germany's treaties with the Soviet Union and Poland.[3]

In West Germany itself, similar positive attitudes were registered in April of 1972. Approximately 57 percent of the population recommended ratification of the latter two treaties as "serving German interests," and 61 percent endorsed Ostpolitik in general. This figure of 61 percent represented a substantial change, for in October 1971, seven months earlier and one month after conclusion of the Quadripartite Agreement, only 53 percent of the West German population had endorsed Ostpolitik; and in the summer of 1971, prior to conclusion of the Quadripartite Agreement, only 42 percent of West Germany's population had endorsed Ostpolitik. Thus, in less than one year, the number of West German citizens who approved the Ostpolitik of Chancellor Brandt's government had increased by almost 40 percent. It was a change which proved to be of enormous significance later in 1972.[4]

While Ostpolitik and the terms of the Berlin agreement were favorably received by the population, the parliamentary debate in West Germany which had focused on Ostpolitik and on the government's position on the Berlin negotiations continued. World attention, however, spotlighted the chancellor himself, who was awarded the Nobel Peace Prize in the autumn for his efforts to improve relations between West Germany and Eastern Europe.

---

[3] See "Infas Report" (Bonn), 17 April 1972 for the results of a public opinion poll taken by the Institut für angewandte Sozialwissenschaft.

[4] Ibid., 17 December 1971 and 3 May 1972.

The foreign policy debate reached its peak in September 1972, a year after the initial agreement. In the spring of 1972, the slim twelve-vote margin enjoyed by the SPD-FDP coalition in the Bundestag had finally evaporated when a sixth member of the coalition left to join the CDU/CSU. The result was a parliamentary stalemate: the CDU/CSU and the SPD-FDP each had 248 representatives in the Bundestag. On 22 September, following rejection of a vote of confidence in Chancellor Brandt's government, the Bundestag was dissolved. New national elections were called for 19 November 1972.

The CDU/CSU opposition waged an election campaign based on criticism of the government for failing to implement promised domestic reforms, for inciting inflation, and for neglecting German interests in Eastern Europe and European unification. While the CDU/CSU concentrated to a degree on domestic issues, it rapidly became clear that the elections were a referendum on Chancellor Brandt's foreign policy— of which the Berlin agreement and West Germany's treaties with the Soviet Union and Poland were a part.

At the beginning of November, the question of Ostpolitik became more acute when the GDR and the Federal Republic initialed a treaty designed to normalize their relations after more than two decades of deepening division. The treaty provided for an exchange of diplomatic representation between Bonn and East Berlin. While it did not affect four-power rights in Berlin and for Germany as a whole, it did approve the applications of both countries for admission to the United Nations, which would follow if the new Bundestag approved the treaty. State Department spokesman John Bray welcomed this treaty on behalf of the United States government as a contribution "to a relaxation of tension in the heart of Europe." The CDU/CSU, however, reserved the right to renegotiate it if elected to office on 19 November. As Le Figaro wrote in Paris on 7 November, the conclusion of the treaty prior to the elections meant that Chancellor Brandt was, in effect, calling on the German electorate "to approve" his conduct of foreign policy.

The election results confirmed public support for the liberal SPD-FDP coalition, as well as for Ostpolitik. The SPD-FDP received a combined total of 54.3 percent of the vote and 272 seats in the Bundestag, a 48-seat majority. The CDU/CSU dropped from 46.1 percent of the vote to 44.8 percent and suffered a loss of 18 seats, from 242 to 224. As the New York Times wrote on 20 November, the West

97

German voters had delivered "an unexpectedly emphatic endorsement of Chancellor Willy Brandt's strenuous efforts to build reconciliation with Eastern Europe." The *Times* concluded that West German voters not only

> welcomed normalization of relations with Moscow and its allies . . . [but] showed that they approved the new agreements aimed at preserving West Berlin in freedom and at increasing their access to relatives and friends in East Germany even if this meant Bonn's recognition at long last of the existence of the Communist ruled German Democratic Republic.

For the first time in the postwar history of Germany the SPD had received more votes (45.9 percent) than the CDU/CSU (44.8 percent). The chancellor's victory was significant. It gave him a strong mandate for another four years, and it indicated, for the present at least, that West Germans and presumably West Berliners too—although the latter had not been able to vote in the election—considered the SPD and FDP to have won the debate on Ostpolitik begun in 1969.

The Compromises

Praise of practical solutions for old problems was well deserved. For the first time since World War II, the agreement established the principle of *Zugang*—unrestricted civilian access between West Berlin and West Germany. And the Soviet Union acknowledged its responsibility for the flow of this traffic.

During the negotiations the Soviet government had attempted to refer discussion of traffic questions to the German Democratic Republic, since this issue was asserted to be in the province of the sovereign government of East Germany. In the 3 September agreement, however, the Soviet Union declared,

> that transit traffic by road, rail and waterways through the territory of the German Democratic Republic of civilian persons and goods between the Western Sectors of Berlin and the Federal Republic of Germany will be unimpeded; that such traffic will be facilitated so as to take place in the most simple and expeditious manner; and that it will receive preferential treatment.[5]

---

[5] Appendix, p. 118. See also *The Berlin Settlement: The Quadripartite Agreement on Berlin and the Supplementary Arrangements* (Bonn: Press and Information Office of the Government of the Federal Republic of Germany, 1972). This book contains the 1972 agreement, all supplementary documents, and a large number of press conferences and speeches explaining the documents.

During the year following the enactment of the agreement, traffic moved without interruption for the first time since the end of the Berlin blockade in 1949.

In return for *Zugang*, the Western powers agreed to reduce the demonstration of federal presence and declared that the Western sectors of Berlin "continue not to be a constituent part of the Federal Republic." The status of the Soviet sector was not mentioned, nor was the quadripartite status of Greater Berlin altered in any way. By not mentioning East Berlin, both the Soviet and East German governments averred that the West accepted East Berlin's ties with the German Democratic Republic.

The West also obtained *Zuordnung*, the recognition of West Berlin's ties with West Germany, in exchange for reducing the demonstration of federal presence and for the implicit acceptance of East Berlin as the capital of the GDR. In view of the limited concessions the West could offer the Soviet Union in exchange for assurance of unimpeded access and recognition of West Berlin's ties with the Federal Republic, the reduction of demonstrative federal presence was an acceptable compromise. The maintenance and development of these ties was of great political and psychological significance to the citizens of West Berlin. Without their development it would be extremely difficult to generate sufficient confidence in the future of West Berlin to attract investment and residents.

What did the reduction in federal presence entail? The agreement prohibited "constitutional or official acts" of the federal president, the federal government, the National Assembly, the Bundesrat, the Bundestag, including their committees and *Fraktionen* (party blocs), and "other state bodies" designed to demonstrate that West Berlin was a Land of West Germany. The term "state bodies" was defined in the agreement to include "the Federal President, the Federal Chancellor, the Federal Cabinet, the Federal Ministers and Ministries, and the branch offices of those Ministries, the Bundesrat and the Bundestag, and all Federal courts." [6] Despite the attempt to be specific, the term "other state bodies" was ambiguous and could be interpreted in various ways. It would seem certain that the election of a federal president in West Berlin, or the holding of Bundestag meetings on the federal budget there, would definitely violate the agreement. What is unclear is the large middle ground having to do with federal ministries and agencies

[6] Appendix, p. 127.

which are either located in West Berlin or have offices there. Should the Soviet Union or East Germany attempt to give the term "other state bodies" an arbitrary definition in the future and assert that the West German government had not adhered to that definition, new harrassment of the autobahns could ensue in protest of the "violation."

The agreement specifically stated that "the existing ties between the Federal Republic and the Western Sectors of Berlin . . . will be maintained and developed. . . ." [7] Therefore, the West agreed only to prohibit acts which demonstrated direct federal authority in West Berlin. The Western powers declared in the Quadripartite Agreement that "Single committees of the Bundesrat and the Bundestag may meet in the Western Sectors of Berlin in connection with maintaining and developing the ties between those Sectors and the Federal Republic of Germany. In the case of Fraktionen, meetings will not be held simultaneously." The Federal Republic was to be represented in West Berlin by the offices of a permanent liaison agency, including "departments charged with liaison functions in their respective fields." This meant that the federal employees working in Berlin would remain at their posts. In fact, by 1973 there were more federal workers in West Berlin than there were in Bonn. [8]

In addition, the Federal Republic could perform "consular services for permanent residents of the Western Sectors of Berlin" and would represent West Berlin in all international agreements that did not concern "matters of security and status." West Germany would also, according to the agreement, represent West Berlin at international organizations and conferences. Permanent residents were invited to "participate jointly with participants from the Federal Republic of Germany in international exchanges and exhibitions." These gatherings could be held in West Berlin.

The agreement also established *Zutritt*. West Berlin citizens would be permitted to visit the Soviet sector and the German Democratic Republic "under conditions comparable to those applying to other persons entering these areas." [9] The official West German interpretation of this statement was issued 3 September 1971.

---

[7] Ibid., p. 129.

[8] In 1973 approximately 24,000 federal officials worked in West Berlin and approximately 22,000 worked in Bonn. See Marion Gräfin Dönhoff, "Weltstadt im Hinterhof?" *Die Zeit,* 30 March 1973.

[9] Appendix, p. 118.

The agreement at last removed for the West Berliners . . .
the unequal treatment in comparison to other persons for
visits to the Eastern part of the city and to the German Democratic Republic. For the first time since the expiration of the
last negotiations for pass agreements in 1966, they have the
possibility on a general and permanent basis to travel to these
areas under conditions that correspond to those for other
persons.[10]

Whether the GDR would make the conditions of *Zutritt* more
difficult in the future for *all* persons, including West Berliners, was
uncertain, since the "conditions" were not specifically defined. For
example, a GDR decision to increase the amount of money visitors are
required to spend on a daily basis in East Berlin or East Germany
would affect West Berliners more seriously than it would West German
citizens—that is, the latter are not required to pay a price for a casual
visit on a weekend to the environs of their cities.[11]

The September agreement also provided for the establishment of a
Soviet consulate general in West Berlin. According to the agreement,
the activities of the consulate general "will be of a consular character
and will not include political functions or any matters related to quadripartite rights or responsibilities." The consulate general would increase
Soviet presence in West Berlin, but its accreditation to the Western
powers emphasized the validity of past quadripartite accords which
governed the position of the Western powers in their respective sectors.
If this consulate general were not to contribute to the establishment of
a four-power status for West Berlin alone, it was important that the
Soviet government not be granted any greater rights of a quadripartite
nature in West Berlin than had been granted in the past.

Problems of Interpretation

Despite the attempts to be specific, the negotiators left areas which may
produce future difficulty. In large measure, likely future problems will

---

[10] See "Das Viermächte-Abkommen über Berlin vom 3. September 1971," *Bulletin,*
no. 127 (Presse- und Informationsamt der Bundesregierung), 3 September 1971.

[11] On 15 November 1973 the amount of money that West Berliners and West
Germans traveling to East Berlin and the GDR were required to spend on a daily
basis was doubled. See the following articles on this issue: Marlies Menge, "Reizt
an Ostberlin der Harzer Käse?" *Die Zeit,* 23 November 1973; "Heating Up Berlin,"
editorial in the *New York Times,* 13 November 1973; Eduard Neumaier, "Bonn
ging auf den Leim," *Die Zeit,* 24 August 1973.

be the same as past problems. In other words, it cannot be guaranteed that the agreement solved the central disputes over Berlin. In particular the agreement is ambiguous about West Berlin's political status and its ties with West Germany.

Although the Soviet Union acknowledged that West Berlin's ties with West Germany will be "maintained and developed," another clause in the agreement stipulates that "the situation which has developed in the area, and as it is defined in this Agreement as well as in the other agreements referred to in this Agreement, shall not be changed unilaterally." The ambiguity of this phrase could well be a source of future difficulty. Essentially the phrase means that the city's four-power status continues to exist, that this status still provides the legal basis for Western presence in their sectors, and that it cannot be altered unilaterally. But the phrase "shall not be changed unilaterally" is not specifically defined. The Soviet or East German governments could interpret it as meaning that no ties with West Germany may be developed which would produce a "unilateral" change in the status of Berlin. This interpretation would, in effect, give the Soviet Union a right to veto measures on West Berlin's internal affairs should the Soviet representatives assert that a given measure would produce a unilateral change.

On West Berlin's status, the agreement expressly states that the four powers concluded the accord "without prejudice to their legal positions," and that their "individual and joint rights and responsibilities . . . remain unchanged." Secretary of State William Rogers said on 3 September 1971 that the West had achieved the objective of "practical improvements in and around the city without altering the status of Berlin or diminishing our rights and responsibilities there." [12] But the fact that agreements were concluded on practical issues does not make those agreements devoid of political content. It remains to be seen whether the Soviet Union would argue that the changes in the practical aspects of Berlin life have, in fact, changed the political situation of the city.

The separation of political and practical problems in Berlin is attributed to Egon Bahr, who was state secretary in the chancellor's office.[13] Bahr had suggested in April 1971 that it was possible for the Soviet Union, France, Great Britain, and the United States each to

---

[12] *New York Times,* 4 September 1971.
[13] *Westfälische Rundschau,* 6 May 1971, and *Frankfurter Allgemeine Zeitung,* 24 April 1971.

adhere to its own interpretation of Berlin's legal and political status while concluding agreements on "humane" and therefore nonpolitical issues. He defined humane issues as the "guarantee of the access roads, settlement of intra-city problems, legal protection for West Berlin residents under the Bonn Basic Law." [14]

Soviet recognition of its responsibilities for access and acknowledgment of West Berlin's ties with the Federal Republic constituted "a clear departure from the earlier demand for [Western recognition] of an 'independent political entity' " of West Berlin.[15] This phrase does not appear in the agreement. Moreover, the German Democratic Republic changed its way of referring to West Berlin during the course of the negotiations from an "independent political entity" to a "city with a special political status." [16] This revision could, however, represent a rewording of the same basic assertion, since many of the passages of the Quadripartite Agreement of 1971 contain ambiguities that present opportunities for different interpretations.

Throughout the negotiations, the Soviet Union and other members of the Warsaw Pact asserted that they were dealing with "the problem of the legal and political status of West Berlin." [17] Despite repeated official Western rejection of this claim, some Western journalists accepted it. Jean Schwoebel, writing for *Le Monde*, suggested that the negotiations were being conducted "to determine once and for all the status of the former German capital." [18] This statement was unfounded. However, the point is not merely that the statement is wrong, but that repetitions of the statement by Western journalists would seem to complicate matters for Western negotiators. It would be difficult for them to reject Soviet assertions if the Soviet Union can buttress the assertions with Western acceptance of their content.

The establishment of the Soviet consulate general in West Berlin could be another complicating matter. Under past quadripartite agreements, the Soviet Union had maintained official presence in each of the Western sectors. It participated in the four-power administration of

---

[14] *Westfälische Rundschau*, 6 May 1971.

[15] Dieter Mahncke, "Das Viermächte-Abkommen über Berlin: Bilanz und Aussichten," *Europa-Archiv*, Series 20 (1971), p. 706.

[16] *Neues Deutschland*, 16 June 1971.

[17] See, for example, an article by J. Wankowicz, Berlin correspondent for the Polish news agency Polska Agencja Prasoxa (PAP), 25 May 1971.

[18] Jean Schwoebel, "Berlin: The Hyphen in East-West Relations," *Le Monde Weekly*, English ed., 13-19 May 1971, p. 4.

the Spandau prison in the French sector and of the Berlin Air Safety Center in the American sector, and it maintained the Soviet War Memorial in the British sector. It may be assumed that the Soviet Union will continue each of these activities.[19] The Western powers on the other hand have no such responsibilities of presence in East Berlin. It is in this context that the establishment of the Soviet consulate general must be evaluated. While its accreditation to the three Western powers recognized past quadripartite agreements, it could nevertheless act as a support for Soviet claims, over the long term, that only West Berlin is under four-power administration and negotiation.

Given the well-known Soviet desire that West Berlin be turned into an independent city or an international city, it is not at all impossible that the Soviet government might assert that its consulate general testifies to West Berlin's "special political status." It is unclear whether the mere presence of the consulate general would support such an assertion. But should the consulate general become indirectly accredited to the West Berlin Senat in addition to formal accreditation with the three Western powers, the Soviet Union will have made a large stride toward proving its case.[20] Other events which might support claims of West Berlin's political independence would be location of Western embassies in East Berlin or the admission of the two German states to the United Nations. Both events have occurred since the enactment of the agreement. And, in fact, neither has undermined the validity of the quadripartite agreements governing Allied occupation of Berlin or Soviet support for West Germany's representation of West Berlin at the United Nations. But they may yet strengthen, from the Soviet viewpoint, a future East German assertion that East Berlin is the sovereign capital of the sovereign state of the German Democratic Republic and that, therefore, the Quadripartite Agreement does not apply to the Soviet sector and is, in reality, a four-power agreement on West Berlin.

One example will demonstrate the potential trouble contained in the ambiguities of the agreement. The provisions state that the agree-

---

[19] This desire to maintain presence in the Western sectors may explain Soviet refusal to approve the release from Spandau prison of the last "war criminal," Rudolf Hess, whose incarceration costs the West German government 850 thousand marks yearly.

[20] In February 1973, the Soviet government asked the Western powers whether it might be practical to permit the consulate general in West Berlin "certain political functions." See Joachim Boelke, "Generalkonsulat als Beispiel," *Der Tagesspiegel*, 28 February 1973 and Joachim Nawrocki, "Zum Tennis in den Dahlemer Klub," *Die Zeit*, 5 April 1974.

ment takes "into acount the existing situation in the relevant area" but fails to define the area in question. However, there is no statement in the agreement that suggests that the agreement pertains solely to the Western sectors. When President Nixon was visiting Secretary Brezhnev in Moscow in May 1972, before the agreement was enacted, the United States and the U.S.S.R. released a joint communiqué that referred to the "quadripartite agreement relating to the Western sectors of Berlin as a good example of faithful cooperation between the states concerned." [21] After the communiqué was released, a State Department spokesman agreed that the phrasing was unfortunate in that it did not mention that East Berlin was part of the agreement. The spokesman argued that the reference to the Western sectors implied the existence of a Soviet sector.[22] Those who drafted the communiqué were reportedly content "that they had brought their Russian counterparts down from a definition of the four-power agreement as dealing solely with 'West Berlin.' " Diplomats suggested that this was nevertheless a gain for the Soviet Union that could cause conflicting interpretation of the quadripartite agreement in the future.

The reference to the "Western sectors" of Berlin in the Nixon-Brezhnev communiqué illustrates well the difficulties that could flow from the use of ambiguous language. It is worth noting that on 3 June, two days following enactment of the agreement, Soviet Foreign Minister Gromyko and First Secretary of the SED Erich Honecker both declared in East Berlin that the Berlin agreement was in reality a "quadripartite agreement on West Berlin." [23]

Although the Soviet Union and the GDR asserted continually during the negotiations that the four powers sought to achieve an agreement on the "West Berlin" question, no statement to this effect is contained in the agreement itself. A quadripartite status for West Berlin alone never existed, and the negotiations did not deal with "West Berlin." Yet, in the general provisions of the agreement, in its four annexes, and in its two agreed minutes, the phrase "Western Sectors of Berlin" appears more than forty separate times, while the word

---

[21] The text of the joint Nixon-Brezhnev communiqué is reprinted in the *New York Times,* 30 May 1972.

[22] David Binder, "East Berlin Role of Big 4 Disputed," ibid., 8 June 1972.

[23] These references were made in speeches delivered at a dinner given Foreign Minister Gromyko by Honecker during a visit by Gromyko to East Berlin on 5 June 1972. They were broadcast by ADN at 1921 and 1944 GMT on 5 June 1972.

"Berlin" does not appear at all. At the same time, however, the four powers reaffirmed in the provisions of the agreement that they were "acting on the basis of their quadripartite rights and responsibilities, and of the corresponding wartime and postwar agreements and decisions of the Four Powers, which are not affected." Since these agreements of 1944-45 and 1949 applied to Greater Berlin and remain valid, even though the city is divided, it is clear that the Quadripartite Agreement of 1971 did not establish a new status for West Berlin. But in view of Soviet and GDR assertions in September of 1971 and in June 1972 that a "Quadripartite Agreement on West Berlin" had been concluded, this question of status remains subject to differing interpretation. In a sense, therefore, the four powers may have agreed to disagree.

At the same time, however, the agreement did produce an immediate improvement in traffic conditions, and there are other areas in which the Quadripartite Agreement has been satisfactory. In the postal agreement concluded between East and West Germany on 30 September 1971 (an agreement which included West Berlin) the German Democratic Republic acknowledges the right of the Federal Republic to negotiate on behalf of the West Berlin government. The treaty concluded between Czechoslovakia and the Federal Republic on 20 June 1973 contains a provision extending its terms to West Berlin in accordance with the Quadripartite Agreement. The two agreements concerning aviation and economic, industrial and technical cooperation between West Germany and the Soviet Union concluded in Moscow in May 1973 include a clause extending the provisions to include West Berlin in accordance with the Quadripartite Agreement.

In addition, in the Basic Treaty between East and West Germany of 8 November 1972, Chancellor Brandt secured East German acceptance that the Federal Republic would represent the interests of West Berlin in the United Nations in accordance with the Quadripartite Agreement. This was a major point. A quadripartite declaration accompanying the treaty and supporting the German application to the United Nations affirms "that this membership shall in no way affect the rights and responsibilities of the four powers and the corresponding related quadripartite agreements, decisions, and practices." [24]

---

[24] *New York Times,* 6 and 10 November 1972.

Détente and Berlin

Lest this analysis be construed to mean that the Quadripartite Agreement of 1971 is unsatisfactory or that the West gave away more than it received, it should be emphasized that the West gained Soviet recognition of *Zugang, Zuordnung,* and *Zutritt.* The Quadripartite Agreement improved the situation in and around Berlin on a basis acceptable to East and West. Moreover, it contributed to the conclusion of treaties between West Germany and the Soviet Union, Poland, Czechoslovakia, and the German Democratic Republic; it contributed to the convening of a conference on European security and cooperation; it has contributed to the discussions on mutual and balanced force reductions in Europe. It has also had the effect of freezing the division of Germany, because it does, in essence, recognize the existence of two German states.

In Berlin the cycle of harassment and demonstration of federal presence—measure for measure—was broken by the agreement, and with that break the character of the cold war changed dramatically. But ideological differences remained. It is clear that the continuance of ideological conflict poses serious difficulties for the stability of peaceful coexistence. It is also clear that the transformation from an era of confrontation to one of cooperation—in Berlin and elsewhere in Europe, and above all between the Soviet Union and the United States—has been decisively influenced by the Quadripartite Agreement on Berlin. Writing for the *Washington Post* following the second Nixon-Brezhnev meeting (late June 1973), Chalmers M. Roberts stated that "the Soviet Union today, for its own reasons which combine the nuclear, economic and political facts of life, is acting more like a country and less like a cause than in past decades." He went on to say, "In part, at least, this is because the United States, especially in the Nixon years, also is acting more like a country and less like a cause." [25]

In his analysis of the Nixon-Brezhnev meeting, Henry Kissinger emphasized on 22 June 1973 that the "principal goal" of the foreign policy of the United States since 1969 "has been to set up what the President has called a structure of peace, by which we mean an international system less geared to the management of crises, less conscious of constant eruptions of conflict, in which the principal participants operate with a consciousness of stability and permanence." He con-

---

[25] "The U.S.-Soviet Thaw," *Washington Post,* 11 July 1973.

107

tinued that President Nixon, "from the day of his first Inauguration, has emphasized that we wanted to move from confrontation to negotiation. And in those negotiations we have operated on many levels. We have attempted to remove specific causes of tension. We have attempted to forge specific instruments of cooperation." [26] Without doubt, one of these instruments was the Quadripartite Agreement of 1971.

Stress has been laid upon the problems of interpreting the agreement, because it would be a serious policy error for the West, just as it would be for the East, to underestimate the significance of these problems and hence not discuss them in relation to Berlin. In the future, the words used to describe the policies and agreements affecting the city will almost certainly be of primary importance. This is because those words will denote the perception of the problem, and the perception dictates future policy judgments. For example, if one accepts the revisionist position on the cold war—that the cause of the Berlin problem was an arrogant and irresponsible American foreign policy— then one would be likely to suggest a different negotiating position from the one the West actually took in the 1970-71 negotiations. And it should be remembered that policy judgment is important because it dictates the approach one takes toward ensuring West Berlin's security.

It is also important that there be no equivocation over the definitions in the agreement. Otherwise the logical conclusion would be that the West is uncertain of its own policy and its own perception of the problems. Any Soviet attempt to interpret the Berlin agreement as an indication that a four-power status has been established for West Berlin alone must be clearly and unambiguously rejected. If it is not, the assertion will be repeated until it becomes the subject of negotiation. Mere Western agreement to discuss such an assertion would accord it legitimacy. It would thus become a precedent requiring compromise settlement because it is a source of disagreement. If it is not understood that the threat to the freedom of Berlin is primarily political, new harassment of the city may be interpreted as warranting new negotiations to preserve détente. That is precisely how it should not be interpreted. Harassment should be interpreted as an instrument employed for the political purpose of gaining new concessions from the West through the process of negotiation. The consequence of such a policy,

---

[26] Excerpts from Kissinger's briefing are reprinted in the *New York Times,* 23 June 1973.

to use Henry Kissinger's phrase of a decade ago, would be "the attrition of Berlin's freedom." [27]

Not only must attention be given to the definition of the problems and to a consistent approach to them, but perspective must be maintained. It must be clear who is responsible for creating the problems that require solution. In an era of détente, major ideological differences will continue to divide East from West. Public opinion can exert tremendous pressure on governments to compromise—a fact observed in the harassment of access to Berlin. By 1970 the question was no longer whether the harassment was illegal but how to stop it. This change was a serious matter. What occurred was simple, although the step-by-step execution was more complicated: the Soviet Union annexed the Soviet sector. It then refused to discuss this violation of the four-power status of Berlin. It asserted instead that there existed a four-power status for West Berlin that, it claimed, was an "independent political entity." By 1970 the Berlin problem had completely altered in scope. The division of Berlin had become so permanent and the transformation of the Soviet sector into the capital of the GDR so complete that negotiation with the Soviet Union on restoring unity to the city was not possible. The West sought, therefore, to gain Soviet recognition that its assertions concerning the Western sectors were invalid and to secure Soviet guarantees for *Zugang, Zuordnung,* and *Zutritt.*[28]

The difficulty was that, as far as the West Berliners were concerned, the issues were day-to-day hassles, not far-removed legal disputes. The solution to these issues did not logically require Western concessions, for the West had not created the problems. Nevertheless, by 1970 concessions were necessary if an agreement was to be reached that was acceptable to all four powers. In the words of one CSU Bundestag member, Karl Theodor Freiherr zu Guttenberg (with whom West Berlin CDU Chairman Peter Lorenz concurred), what really had taken place was this: "that which is characterized as concessions of the Soviet Union . . . is in reality the partial return to the West of rights that have been pilfered in the past years." [29]

---

[27] Henry Kissinger, *The Necessity for Choice* (New York: Harper and Row, 1961), pp. 140-145.

[28] Cf. my analysis of the annexation of the Soviet sector and the ensuing isolation of West Berlin in *Die Berlin-Frage 1949-1955.*

[29] *Der Spiegel,* 6 September 1971, pp. 23-24. See also Karl Theodor Freiherr zu Guttenberg, *Fussnoten* (Stuttgart: Seewald Verlag, 1971) and Dieter Mahncke, *Berlin im geteilten Deutschland* (Munich: R. Oldenbourg Verlag, 1973).

One year after the conclusion of West Germany's treaty with the Soviet Union, State Secretary Egon Bahr expressed his belief that "in its practical behavior" the Soviet Union "accepted the fact that improvements in the relations between our two states and détente in central Europe cannot become effective while the threat of permanent friction or crisis continues to exist in and around Berlin." [30] But Bahr could not guarantee that the Berlin agreement had removed "the threat of permanent friction or crisis." The Soviet government had harassed Berlin for so long that any agreement bringing respite could be interpreted as an indication that the U.S.S.R. sought genuine détente with the West.

President Nixon said in February 1972 that the agreement could indeed terminate "the use of the citizens of West Berlin as Cold War hostages, and . . . reduce the danger of Berlin once again becoming the focus of a sharp and dangerous international confrontation." The President also cautioned that "agreements are not . . . an end in themselves." They can have "permanent significance only when they contribute to a stable structure of peace." [31]

It cannot be emphasized too strongly that this stable structure can only exist when there is a common perception of European conditions and mutual recognition of the programs necessary to alleviate commonly perceived problems. If the possibility of differing interpretations is discounted or ignored, a deceptive psychological atmosphere could develop. If old problems concerning the status of Berlin should recur or, for example, if new harassment of the access ways should develop, those caught in their self-deceptions would find themselves in a difficult position. They would face the alternatives of either asserting that new negotiation and new concession would solve new problems or of suddenly insisting on consistent interpretation of past agreements. This applies particularly to those who did not heed Ambassador Abrasimov's interpretation of peaceful coexistence at the opening of the negotiations. On 1 April 1970, in an article in *Neues Deutschland,* the ambassador defined peaceful coexistence to be the continuation of "class struggle in the international arena," and drew the conclusion that "peaceful coexistence is a dialectical phenomenon which contains elements of cooperation as well as elements of conflict."

---

[30] *Süddeutsche Zeitung,* 11 August 1971.

[31] Richard M. Nixon, "United States Foreign Policy for the 1970s," pp. 4-5.

Berlin and a Stable Structure of Peace

Since 1949 the presence of the Western garrisons has provided the best assurance that West Berlin would not be subject to military attack. The Quadripartite Agreement on Berlin has greatly reduced tensions in and around the city, thereby establishing a relatively stable political atmosphere. This atmosphere aids the chances of economic prosperity and thus fulfills a primary requirement for West Berlin's survival as a free city.

As long as the military defense of Berlin remains credible and the Quadripartite Agreement is observed by all parties (including East and West Germany), the potential for future crises should remain low. But as Chancellor Brandt observed in his letter to President Nixon on 5 September 1971, the Berlin problem will not be solved until a solution has been found for the German question.[32] This means that a careful program to strengthen West Berlin's economy will probably not be sufficient, in and of itself, to ensure the city's continued economic viability as long as there is political uncertainty about the city's relation to the Federal Republic.

With growing East-West cooperation it is likely that the necessity for continuing defense of the city will be subject to question. Significant progress in discussions on mutual and balanced troop reductions in Europe or in the conference on European security and cooperation would strengthen those asking the questions. If old adversaries draw closer together, the justification for large military expenditures—in this case, for the stationing of troops in West Berlin—could become subject to increasing criticism, even though Germany remains divided.

The change in Senator Mike Mansfield's position on maintaining American troops in Europe is indicative of changing political judgment. In 1962 the senator maintained that the single factor that explained America's undertaking "the great costs and risks" in the defense of Berlin was "the basic concept of all-German unification in peace." He saw "no alternative to the continuance of the Berlin commitment." It was necessary to hold such a commitment because the maintenance of a free Berlin, he said, was "interrelated with the future of freedom in Europe and the peace of the world." [33]

---

[32] The text of the letter is printed in *Bulletin,* no. 128 (Presse- und Informationsamt der Bundesregierung, 7 September 1971).

[33] U.S. Senate Committee on Foreign Relations, "Berlin in a Changing Europe" (Washington, D.C.: Government Printing Office, 1963), pp. 5-8.

But in the early 1970s it was Senator Mansfield who questioned the justification for maintaining American troops in Europe. The change in his position suggested a number of complex questions. Although "a free Berlin" was not questioned, did the "Berlin commitment" remain the same? In other words, Senator Mansfield's change implicitly questioned the need for maintaining troops in Berlin in order to maintain a free Berlin. This, of course, reflected a changing appraisal of Soviet foreign policy. Was it still a Soviet goal to assimilate West Berlin into the German Democratic Republic? Did the West still wish to maintain the posture that European freedom and peace were inextricably connected to the fate of Berlin? If peaceful coexistence was in fact achieved, would a reduction of troops actually make Europe safer? Senator Mansfield was suggesting that, in view of the successful West German-Soviet agreements, American troops in Europe should be reduced to a "symbolic contingent" of 50,000 men.

It is in this milieu that one must encounter difficulty in assuring businessmen that there is absolutely no question that Berlin could ever be separated from West Germany. After all, as Charles de Gaulle noted when he withdrew from NATO, no alliance is permanent.

One must in fact look at the problem of ensuring West Berlin's security on a day-to-day basis. Day-to-day concerns are the business of local governments and the problem of the city's security devolves on the West Berlin government. If the West Berlin government is led with imagination and confidence, West Berlin should grow and prosper. The city will certainly need outside help, but its security must be built from within. It may be necessary to direct as much attention to the economic and cultural development of the city in the future as was directed to its military defense in the past.

One year after the agreement's enactment harassment of the access ways was all but eliminated. For the period of June through August 1972, traffic by all forms of access had increased by 35 percent over the same period a year before. Between the time the agreement was enacted and 20 March 1973, more than three million visits were made by West Berliners to East Berlin and East Germany. But, most important, the city's ties with the Federal Republic and with the West as a whole have been maintained and developed. These same ties preserved Berlin's freedom in the past and permitted the Allies to negotiate the Berlin agreement from a strong political position.

The importance of this last point was emphasized by United States Ambassador to the Federal Republic Martin J. Hillenbrand in September 1972. In his view, increased investment and smooth passenger and freight traffic to and from Berlin would not only have beneficial effects on the city's economy, but would also make the city "even more secure as its manifold ties to the Federal Republic continue to be developed." [34]

One approach to developing West Berlin's ties with West Germany as well as with other countries is to stage events in the city—events such as agricultural, trade, and industrial fairs. The city has been hosting fairs for years. Congresses and exhibitions held in West Berlin during 1972 were attended by representatives from Eastern European countries, the Soviet Union, and the People's Republic of China. More than twenty major fairs, exhibits, and congresses were scheduled in West Berlin during 1973. Among the more important fairs held regularly in West Berlin are the "International Green Week" (which is the largest display of agricultural products in Europe), the convention of the International Tourism Exchange, the convention of the German Developing Countries Foundation, and the "Partners for Progress" Overseas Import Fair, at which the countries of Latin America, Africa, and Asia exhibit their wares.

Investment by multinational corporations in West Berlin has continued to increase. International Business Machines, Litton Industries, and General Motors have production operations in West Berlin. Gillette, Otis Elevator, Warner-Lambert, Continental Can, Kaiser Aluminum, National Cash Register, and Standard Electric Lorenze division of International Telephone and Telegraph also have works in the city. Two large German-based multinational industries, Siemens and AEG-Telefunken, produced close to $1 billion worth of goods in the city in 1972. Almost one billion West German marks are being invested in West Berlin's manufacturing industries every year. American companies account for almost 7 percent of the city's industrial turnover and for approximately 15 percent of the investment. The presence of these corporations and their investments in the city should demonstrate the city's potential for economic strength.[35]

[34] United States ambassador to West Germany, Martin J. Hillenbrand, in an address delivered on 14 September 1972 to members of the German World Economic Association in West Berlin. *Bulletin,* no. 31, 26 September 1972, and *Der Tagesspiegel,* 22 and 23 March 1973.
[35] *Berlin Business Barometer,* vol. 5, no. 1, 1973.

The federal government provides subsidies and other financial preferences which play major roles in making up the city's budget deficit. In 1973 federal assistance amounted to almost 4.5 billion West German marks. In 1951 the figure had been 550 million marks. This aid will continue to be necessary.

To attract the increasing numbers of tourists the city will need for income, it will have to help develop its architecture, shops, museums, restaurants, galleries, theaters, music, and universities. Many of its establishments are already world-renowned. Its freeway rings and apartment complexes like the Märkisches-Viertal, the Gropiusstadt, and the Hansa-Viertal are widely studied for their contribution to city planning. West Berlin's restaurants and theaters have long been well known. And although its universities have experienced severe political and educational difficulties since 1967, they too could again become models for higher education and advanced research.[36]

Another project that could be undertaken to develop the city's position and ties with the West is the establishment of a European academy of sciences in the city. Or the European Parliament could meet more frequently there. The European Cartel Bureau could be located in West Berlin. Since this group would be active in trading with the East, it would develop the city's ties with Eastern Europe. As Mayor Schütz has pointed out, there is "no place more ideally suited for peaceful interchange between Eastern Europe and the Common Market" than Berlin.[37]

There is no more suitable geographic location for a *Drehscheibe* (turntable) or "bridge" between East and West on the continent. Of course, to make Berlin into a *Drehscheibe* would require not only further development of the city's ties with the West but also an Eastern desire to establish West Berlin as a bridge. It is true that increased cooperation can be in the mutual and individual interests of the nations of East and West. Eastern Europe requires economic assistance and technological know-how from the West. For the West, increased contact offers the hope, at least, of gradual change in the structure of totalitarian regimes. For both East and West, greater cooperation can yield

---

[36] This is a particularly complicated issue. The problems are discussed in some depth in Jürgen Domes, "What Freedom Is Left at the Berlin Free University?" *Central Europe Journal* (July/August 1972), pp. 267-271; and Dennis L. Bark, "Impressions of Student Life in Germany Today," ibid., pp. 257-267.

[37] *Relay from Bonn,* 22 December 1971. For similar remarks of a later date see *Der Spiegel,* 3 January 1972 and *Relay from Bonn,* 7 February 1972.

more stable relationships and can lessen the possibility of future conflict. There is a realistic balance that can be achieved.

Increased economic contact between Eastern and Western Europe has been welcomed by the majority of the Eastern European states. Economic, cultural, scientific and technical exchange between East and West in Europe has been developing at a rapid pace since 1970. Since the enactment of the Berlin agreement in 1972, this development has also applied to West Berlin. If time, effort, and an era of détente permit West Berlin to become a "city of Europe" and a "bridge" between East and West on the continent, a major step toward preserving peace —or even an uncontested reality in the middle of divided Europe— would have taken place.

At the same time, however, the transformation of West Berlin into a "bridge" between East and West would be a lengthy process. As long as West Berlin remains free and its economic prosperity increases, its existence will remind the citizens of totalitarian states that democracy is possible. Thus, there will continue to be great pressure on the governments of Eastern Europe to keep West Berlin isolated. This is, after all, one of the purposes of the Berlin Wall—which continues to stand, just as mine fields continue to divide Germany.

If Western support for West Berlin falters, it becomes less likely that the governments of Eastern Europe will contribute to building a bridge in Berlin. They are more likely to remain passive until the threat to West Berlin's security is no longer fresh in the minds of those who determine Western policy. Then they might well encourage the establishment of an independent West Berlin and propose that this "independent political entity" become the bridge. Under such circumstances Eastern cooperation would be of dubious value: West Berlin's freedom would almost certainly have vanished before the bridge would be proposed, if the historical fate of other independent or international cities is used as a measure.

West Berlin's well-known theater critic, Friedrich Luft, has emphasized that there is " 'a new generation arising, more demanding and more enthusiastic. . . . Something's cooking everywhere in Berlin.' " [38] Luft's

---

[38] This quotation is taken from Walter Henry Nelson, *Berliners* (New York: David McKay, 1969), p. 419. See also the following articles on the future of Berlin: Heinrich Lummer, "Das Berlin-Abkommen im Rahmen einer neuen Ostpolitik" (unpublished manuscript, Berlin, September 1971); "Berlin, was nun?" *Zeit Magazin,* November 1971; Martin Kriele, "Können die Berliner sicherer leben?" *Die Zeit,* 22 February 1972; Hans Dornbrach, "West Berlin's Future Continues to Lie with the West," *Nordwest Zeitung,* 16 June 1972; "Berlin '72"

conclusion is one reason why the future of West Berlin is promising. Spirit and character have made West Berlin one of the most unusual and complex cities in Europe. If the Western nations can maintain their guard and if the Eastern nations can find an acceptable accommodation with the West, the promise of West Berlin's future can become a reality.

For these reasons, the motives for past attempts to undermine the confidence of West Berliners in their future should not be forgotten, notwithstanding assurances in both Eastern and Western Europe that the "cold war" is at an end. Both the hope for and the threat to West Berlin lie in the passage of time, and therefore it must be continually stressed in the West that the city's freedom is worth preserving, just as its enemies agree that its freedom is worth attacking. On 15 June 1973, West Germany's Foreign Minister Walter Scheel emphasized that in the future Berlin will be "a symbol for the degree of détente in Europe." [39] Just as the introduction of an era of negotiation on the continent depended to a major degree on the satisfactory conclusion of the 1971 Quadripartite Agreement, the measure of that agreement will also very likely rise and fall according to the dilemmas of détente and peaceful coexistence elsewhere in Europe.

The problem of Berlin has not been solved, but the situation has been greatly improved. Tensions have been reduced and the burdens of isolation have been eased. The protracted negotiations leading to the Quadripartite Agreement of 1971 delineated many of the problems and issues that may be encountered in future East/West relations. As these relations develop, the future of West Berlin will continue to present a challenge for diplomatic settlement. West Berlin will remain a key to the future of Germany as Germany is a key to Europe— not least because, after nearly thirty years as a focus of contention, it remains a living city.

(with contributions by Rüdiger Altmann, Günter Grass, Dieter Hildebrandt, Richard Löwenthal, Matthias Walden), *Christ und Welt,* 7 July 1972; Marion Gräfin Dönhoff, "Weltstadt im Hinterhof?" *Die Zeit,* 30 March 1973; Henk Petersen, "Miese Stimmung," *Die Zeit,* 5 October 1973; Arturo F. Gonzalez, Jr., and Ellen Lentz, "Achtung! Berlin Is Becoming a Fun City. Haven't You Heard?" *New York Times,* 7 October 1973; "Das Recht mit Festigkeit vertreten: Ein Zeit-Gespräch mit dem Regierenden Bürgermeister von Berlin Klaus Schütz," *Die Zeit,* 23 November 1973; "Berlin Environment," an editorial in the *New York Times,* 25 January 1974; David K. Willis, "West Berlin: Beneath the Glitter . . . .," *Christian Science Monitor,* 22 February 1974; Craig R. Whitney, "Berlin Is a Puzzle That Blends Tension with Bustle and Decay," *New York Times,* 23 February 1974.
[39] *Relay from Bonn,* 18 June 1973.

Appendix

TEXT OF THE QUADRIPARTITE AGREEMENT OF 3 SEPTEMBER 1971 AND ACCOMPANYING DOCUMENTS*

Quadripartite Agreement

The Governments of the United States of America, the French Republic, the Union of Soviet Socialist Republics, and the United Kingdom of Great Britain and Northern Ireland,

Represented by their Ambassadors, who held a series of meetings in the building formerly occupied by the Allied Control Council in the American Sector of Berlin,

Acting on the basis of their quadripartite rights and responsibilities, and of the corresponding wartime and postwar agreements and decisions of the Four Powers, which are not affected,

Taking into account the existing situation in the relevant area,

Guided by the desire to contribute to practical improvements of the situation,

Without prejudice to their legal positions,

Have agreed on the following:

Part I

General Provisions

1. The four Governments will strive to promote the elimination of tension and the prevention of complications in the relevant area.

2. The four Governments, taking into account their obligations under the Charter of the United Nations, agree that there shall be no use or threat of force in the area and that disputes shall be settled solely by peaceful means.

---

*Source: U.S., Department of State, Publication 8620, *Current Foreign Policy; Berlin: the Four Power Agreement,* European and British Commonwealth Series, no. 73 (1971), pp. 10-14.

117

3. The four Governments will mutually respect their individual and joint rights and responsibilities, which remain unchanged.

4. The four Governments agree that, irrespective of the differences in legal views, the situation which has developed in the area, and as it is defined in this Agreement as well as in the other agreements referred to in this Agreement, shall not be changed unilaterally.

Part II

Provisions Relating to the Western Sectors of Berlin

A. The Government of the Union of Soviet Socialist Republics declares that transit traffic by road, rail and waterways through the territory of the German Democratic Republic of civilian persons and goods between the Western Sectors of Berlin and the Federal Republic of Germany will be unimpeded; that such traffic will be facilitated so as to take place in the most simple and expeditious manner; and that it will receive preferential treatment.

Detailed arrangements concerning this civilian traffic, as set forth in Annex I, will be agreed by the competent German authorities.

B. The Governments of the French Republic, the United Kingdom and the United States of America declare that the ties between the Western Sectors of Berlin and the Federal Republic of Germany will be maintained and developed, taking into account that these Sectors continue not to be a constituent part of the Federal Republic of Germany and not to be governed by it.

Detailed arrangements concerning the relationship between the Western Sectors of Berlin and the Federal Republic of Germany are set forth in Annex II.

C. The Government of the Union of Soviet Socialist Republics declares that communications between the Western Sectors of Berlin and areas bordering on these Sectors and those areas of the German Democratic Republic which do not border on these Sectors will be improved. Permanent residents of the Western Sectors of Berlin will be able to travel to and visit such areas for compassionate, family, religious, cultural or commercial reasons, or as tourists, under conditions comparable to those applying to other persons entering these areas.

The problems of the small enclaves, including Steinstuecken, and of other small areas may be solved by exchange of territory.

Detailed arrangements concerning travel, communications and the exchange of territory, as set forth in Annex III, will be agreed by the competent German authorities.

118

D. Representation abroad of the interests of the Western Sectors of Berlin and consular activities of the Union of Soviet Socialist Republics in the Western Sectors of Berlin can be exercised as set forth in Annex IV.

Part III

Final Provisions

This Quadripartite Agreement will enter into force on the date specified in a Final Quadripartite Protocol to be concluded when the measures envisaged in Part II of this Quadripartite Agreement and in its Annexes have been agreed.

Done at the building formerly occupied by the Allied Control Council in the American Sector of Berlin this 3rd day of September 1971, in four originals, each in the English, French and Russian languages, all texts being equally authentic.

For the Government of the United States
of America:

Kenneth Rush.

For the Government of the French Republic:

Jean Sauvagnargues.

For the Government of the Union of Soviet
Socialist Republics:

Pyotr A. Abrasimov.

For the Government of the United Kingdom
of Great Britain and Northern Ireland:

Roger Jackling.

Annex I

Communication From the Government of the Union of Soviet Socialist Republics to the Governments of the French Republic, the United Kingdom and the United States of America

The Government of the Union of Soviet Socialist Republics, with reference to Part II (A) of the Quadripartite Agreement of this date and after consultation and agreement with the Government of the German Democratic Republic, has the honor to inform the Governments of the French Republic, the United Kingdom and the United States of America that:

1. Transit traffic by road, rail and waterways through the territory of the German Democratic Republic of civilian persons and goods between the Western Sectors of Berlin and the Federal Republic of

119

Germany will be facilitated and unimpeded. It will receive the most simple, expeditious and preferential treatment provided by international practice.

2. Accordingly,

(a) Conveyances sealed before departure may be used for the transport of civilian goods by road, rail and waterways between the Western Sectors of Berlin and the Federal Republic of Germany. Inspection procedures will be limited to the inspection of seals and accompanying documents.

(b) With regard to conveyances which cannot be sealed, such as open trucks, inspection procedures will be limited to the inspection of accompanying documents. In special cases where there is sufficient reason to suspect that unsealed conveyances contain either material intended for dissemination along the designated routes or persons or material put on board along these routes, the content of unsealed conveyances may be inspected. Procedures for dealing with such cases will be agreed by the competent German authorities.

(c) Through trains and buses may be used for travel between the Western Sectors of Berlin and the Federal Republic of Germany. Inspection procedures will not include any formalities other than identification of persons.

(d) Persons identified as through travellers using individual vehicles between the Western Sectors of Berlin and the Federal Republic of Germany on routes designated for through traffic will be able to proceed to their destinations without paying individual tolls and fees for the use of the transit routes. Procedures applied for such travellers shall not involve delay. The travellers, their vehicles and personal baggage will not be subject to search, detention or exclusion from use of the designated routes, except in special cases, as may be agreed by the competent German authorities, where there is sufficient reason to suspect that misuse of the transit routes is intended for purposes not related to direct travel to and from the Western Sectors of Berlin and contrary to generally applicable regulations concerning public order.

(e) Appropriate compensation for fees and tolls and for other costs related to traffic on the communication routes between the Western Sectors of Berlin and the Federal Republic of Germany, including the maintenance of adequate routes, facilities and installations used for such traffic, may be made in the form of an annual lump sum paid to the German Democratic Republic by the Federal Republic of Germany.

3. Arrangements implementing and supplementing the provisions of paragraphs 1 and 2 above will be agreed by the competent German authorities.

Annex II

Communication From the Governments of the French Republic, the United Kingdom and the United States of America to the Government of the Union of Soviet Socialist Republics

The Governments of the French Republic, the United Kingdom and the United States of America, with reference to Part II (B) of the Quadripartite Agreement of this date and after consultation with the Government of the Federal Republic of Germany, have the honor to inform the Government of the Union of Soviet Socialist Republics that:

1. They declare, in the exercise of their rights and responsibilities, that the ties between the Western Sectors of Berlin and the Federal Republic of Germany will be maintained and developed, taking into account that these Sectors continue not to be a constituent part of the Federal Republic of Germany and not to be governed by it. The provisions of the Basic Law of the Federal Republic of Germany and of the Constitution operative in the Western Sectors of Berlin which contradict the above have been suspended and continue not to be in effect.

2. The Federal President, the Federal Government, the Bundesversammlung, the Bundesrat and the Bundestag, including their Committees and Fraktionen, as well as other state bodies of the Federal Republic of Germany will not perform in the Western Sectors of Berlin constitutional or official acts which contradict the provisions of paragraph 1.

3. The Government of the Federal Republic of Germany will be represented in the Western Sectors of Berlin to the authorities of the three Governments and to the Senat by a permanent liaison agency.

Annex III

Communication From the Government of the Union of Soviet Socialist Republics to the Governments of the French Republic, the United Kingdom and the United States of America

The Government of the Union of Soviet Socialist Republics, with reference to Part II (C) of the Quadripartite Agreement of this date and after consultation and agreement with the Government of the German Democratic Republic, has the honor to inform the Governments of the French Republic, the United Kingdom and the United States of America that:

1. Communications between the Western Sectors of Berlin and areas bordering on these Sectors and those areas of the German Democratic Republic which do not border on these Sectors will be improved.

2. Permanent residents of the Western Sectors of Berlin will be able to travel to and visit such areas for compassionate, family, religious, cultural or commercial reasons, or as tourists, under conditions comparable to those applying to other persons entering these areas. In order to facilitate visits and travel, as described above, by permanent residents of the Western Sectors of Berlin, additional crossing points will be opened.

3. The problems of the small enclaves, including Steinstuecken, and of other small areas may be solved by exchange of territory.

4. Telephonic, telegraphic, transport and other external communications of the Western Sectors of Berlin will be expanded.

5. Arrangements implementing and supplementing the provisions of paragraphs 1 to 4 above will be agreed by the competent German authorities.

Annex IV

A. Communication From the Governments of the French Republic, the United Kingdom and the United States of America to the Government of the Union of Soviet Socialist Republics

The Governments of the French Republic, the United Kingdom and the United States of America, with reference to Part II (D) of the Quadripartite Agreement of this date and after consultation with the Government of the Federal Republic of Germany, have the honor to inform the Government of the Union of Soviet Socialist Republics that:

1. The Governments of the French Republic, the United Kingdom and the United States of America maintain their rights and responsibilities relating to the representation abroad of the interests of the Western Sectors of Berlin and their permanent residents, including those rights and responsibilities concerning matters of security and status, both in international organizations and in relations with other countries.

2. Without prejudice to the above and provided that matters of security and status are not affected, they have agreed that:

(a) The Federal Republic of Germany may perform consular services for permanent residents of the Western Sectors of Berlin.

122

(b) In accordance with established procedures, international agreements and arrangements entered into by the Federal Republic of Germany may be extended to the Western Sectors of Berlin provided that the extension of such agreements and arrangements is specified in each case.

(c) The Federal Republic of Germany may represent the interests of the Western Sectors of Berlin in international organizations and international conferences.

(d) Permanent residents of the Western Sectors of Berlin may participate jointly with participants from the Federal Republic of Germany in international exchanges and exhibitions. Meetings of international organizations and international conferences as well as exhibitions with international participation may be held in the Western Sectors of Berlin. Invitations will be issued by the Senat or jointly by the Federal Republic of Germany and the Senat.

3. The three Governments authorize the establishment of a Consulate General of the USSR in the Western Sectors of Berlin accredited to the appropriate authorities of the three Governments in accordance with the usual procedures applied in those Sectors, for the purpose of performing consular services, subject to provisions set forth in a separate document of this date.

B. Communication From the Government of the Union of Soviet Socialist Republics to the Governments of the French Republic, the United Kingdom and the United States of America

The Government of the Union of Soviet Socialist Republics, with reference to Part II (D) of the Quadripartite Agreement of this date and to the communication of the Governments of the French Republic, the United Kingdom and the United States of America with regard to the representation abroad of the interests of the Western Sectors of Berlin and their permanent residents, has the honor to inform the Governments of the French Republic, the United Kingdom and the United States of America that:

1. The Government of the Union of Soviet Socialist Republics takes note of the fact that the three Governments maintain their rights and responsibilities relating to the representation abroad of the interests of the Western Sectors of Berlin and their permanent residents, including those rights and responsibilities concerning matters of security and status, both in international organizations and in relations with other countries.

2. Provided that matters of security and status are not affected, for its part it will raise no objection to:

(a) the performance by the Federal Republic of Germany of consular services for permanent residents of the Western Sectors of Berlin;

(b) in accordance with established procedures, the extension to the Western Sectors of Berlin of international agreements and arrangements entered into by the Federal Republic of Germany provided that the extension of such agreements and arrangements is specified in each case;

(c) the representation of the interests of the Western Sectors of Berlin by the Federal Republic of Germany in international organizations and international conferences;

(d) the participation jointly with participants from the Federal Republic of Germany of permanent residents of the Western Sectors of Berlin in international exchanges and exhibitions, or the holding in those Sectors of meetings of international organizations and international conferences as well as exhibitions with international participation, taking into account that invitations will be issued by the Senat or jointly by the Federal Republic of Germany and the Senat.

3. The Government of the Union of Soviet Socialist Republics takes note of the fact that the three Governments have given their consent to the establishment of a Consulate General of the USSR in the Western Sectors of Berlin. It will be accredited to the appropriate authorities of the three Governments, for purposes and subject to provisions described in their communication and as set forth in a separate document of this date.

Agreed Minute I [1]

It is understood that permanent residents of the Western Sectors of Berlin shall, in order to receive at appropriate Soviet offices visas for entry into the Union of Soviet Socialist Republics, present:

(a) a passport stamped "Issued in accordance with the Quadripartite Agreement of September 3, 1971";

(b) an identity card or other appropriately drawn up document confirming that the person requesting the visa is a permanent resident of the Western Sectors of Berlin and containing the bearer's full address and a personal photograph.

---

[1] Initialed by the four Ambassadors on Sept. 3.

During his stay in the Union of Soviet Socialist Republics, a permanent resident of the Western Sectors of Berlin who has received a visa in this way may carry both documents or either of them, as he chooses. The visa issued by a Soviet office will serve as the basis for entry into the Union of Soviet Socialist Republics, and the passport or identity card will serve as the basis for consular services in accordance with the Quadripartite Agreement during the stay of that person in the territory of the Union of Soviet Socialist Republics.

The above-mentioned stamp will appear in all passports used by permanent residents of the Western Sectors of Berlin for journeys to such countries as may require it.

Agreed Minute II [1]

Provision is hereby made for the establishment of a Consulate General of the USSR in the Western Sectors of Berlin. It is understood that the details concerning this Consulate General will include the following. The Consulate General will be accredited to the appropriate authorities of the three Governments in accordance with the usual procedures applying in those Sectors. Applicable Allied and German legislation and regulations will apply to the Consulate General. The activities of the Consulate General will be of a consular character and will not include political functions or any matters related to quadripartite rights or responsibilities.

The three Governments are willing to authorize an increase in Soviet commercial activities in the Western Sectors of Berlin as described below. It is understood that pertinent Allied and German legislation and regulations will apply to these activities. This authorization will be extended indefinitely, subject to compliance with the provisions outlined herein. Adequate provision for consultation will be made. This increase will include establishment of an "Office of Soviet Foreign Trade Associations in the Western Sectors of Berlin", with commercial status, authorized to buy and sell on behalf of foreign trade associations of the Union of Soviet Socialist Republics. Soyuzpushnina, Prodintorg and Novoexport may each establish a bonded warehouse in the Western Sectors of Berlin to provide storage and display for their goods. The activities of the Intourist office in the British Sector of Berlin may be expanded to include the sale of tickets and vouchers for travel and tours in the Union of Soviet Socialist Republics and other countries. An office of Aeroflot may be established for the sale of passenger tickets and air freight services.

The assignment of personnel to the Consulate General and to permitted Soviet commercial organizations will be subject to agreement with the appropriate authorities of the three Governments. The number of such personnel will not exceed twenty Soviet nationals in the Consulate General; twenty in the office of the Soviet Foreign Trade Associations; one each in the bonded warehouses; six in the Intourist office; and five in the Aeroflot office. The personnel of the Consulate General and of permitted Soviet commercial organizations and their dependents may reside in the Western Sectors of Berlin upon individual authorization.

The property of the Union of Soviet Socialist Republics at Lietzenburgerstrasse 11 and at Am Sandwerder 1 may be used for purposes to be agreed between appropriate representatives of the three Governments and of the Government of the Union of Soviet Socialist Republics.

Details of implementation of the measures above and a time schedule for carrying them out will be agreed between the four Ambassadors in the period between the signature of the Quadripartite Agreement and the signature of the Final Quadripartite Protocol envisaged in that Agreement.

Exchange of Notes

Note From the Three Ambassadors to the Ambassador of the U.S.S.R.[2]

The Ambassadors of the French Republic, the United Kingdom of Great Britain and Northern Ireland and the United States of America have the honor, with reference to the statements contained in Annex II of the Quadripartite Agreement to be signed on this date concerning the relationship between the Federal Republic of Germany and the Western Sectors of Berlin, to inform the Ambassador of the Union of Soviet Socialist Republics of their intention to send to the Chancellor of the Federal Republic of Germany immediately following signature of the Quadripartite Agreement a letter containing clarifications and interpretations which represent the understanding of their Governments of the statements contained in Annex II of the Quadripartite Agreement. A copy of the letter to be sent to the Chancellor of the Federal Republic of Germany is attached to this Note.

The Ambassadors avail themselves of this opportunity to renew to the Ambassador of the Union of Soviet Socialist Republics the assurances of their highest consideration.

Jean Sauvagnargues.

Roger Jackling.

Kenneth Rush.

September 3, 1971.

---

[2] Handed to the Ambassador of the U.S.S.R. prior to the signing of the agreement.

Attachment to Three-Power Note [3]

His Excellency
The Chancellor of the
Federal Republic of Germany,
Bonn.

Your Excellency: With reference to the Quadripartite Agreement signed on September 3, 1971, our Governments wish by this letter to inform the Government of the Federal Republic of Germany of the following clarifications and interpretations of the statements contained in Annex II, which was the subject of consultation with the Government of the Federal Republic of Germany during the quadripartite negotiations.

These clarifications and interpretations represent the understanding of our Governments of this part of the Quadripartite Agreement, as follows:

a. The phrase in Paragraph 2 of Annex II of the Quadripartite Agreement which reads: ". . . will not perform in the Western Sectors of Berlin constitutional or official acts which contradict the provisions of Paragraph 1" shall be interpreted to mean acts in exercise of direct state authority over the Western Sectors of Berlin.

b. Meetings of the Bundesversammlung will not take place and plenary sessions of the Bundesrat and the Bundestag will continue not to take place in the Western Sectors of Berlin. Single committees of the Bundesrat and the Bundestag may meet in the Western Sectors of Berlin in connection with maintaining and developing the ties between those Sectors and the Federal Republic of Germany. In the case of Fraktionen, meetings will not be held simultaneously.

c. The liaison agency of the Federal Government in the Western Sectors of Berlin includes departments charged with liaison functions in their respective fields.

d. Established procedures concerning the applicability to the Western Sectors of Berlin of legislation of the Federal Republic of Germany shall remain unchanged.

e. The term "state bodies" in Paragraph 2 of Annex II shall be interpreted to mean: the Federal President, the Federal Chancellor, the Federal Cabinet, the Federal Ministers and Ministries, and the branch offices of those Ministries, the Bundesrat and the Bundestag, and all Federal courts.

Accept, Excellency, the renewed assurance of our highest esteem.

For the Government of the French Republic:

---

[3] The letter was delivered to the Chancellor of the Federal Republic of Germany on Sept. 3.

For the Government of the United Kingdom
of Great Britain and Northern Ireland:

For the Government of the United States
of America:

Reply From the Ambassador of the U.S.S.R.[4]

Translation

The Ambassador of the Union of Soviet Socialist Republics has the
honor to acknowledge receipt of the note of the Ambassadors of the
French Republic, the United Kingdom of Great Britain and Northern
Ireland, and the United States of America, dated September 3, 1971, and
takes cognizance of the communication of the three Ambassadors.

The Ambassador avails himself of this opportunity to renew to the
Ambassadors of the French Republic, the United Kingdom, and the
United States of America the assurance of his very high consideration.

Pyotr A. Abrasimov.

September 3, 1971.

France–U.S.–U.K. Letter to the Chancellor of the Federal Republic of Germany

September 3, 1971.

His Excellency
The Chancellor of the
Federal Republic of Germany,
Bonn.

Your Excellency: We have the honor by means of this letter to convey
to the Government of the Federal Republic of Germany the text of the
Quadripartite Agreement signed this day in Berlin. The Quadripartite
Agreement was concluded by the Four Powers in the exercise of their
rights and responsibilities with respect to Berlin.

We note that, pursuant to the terms of the Agreement and of the
Final Quadripartite Protocol which ultimately will bring it into force,
the text of which has been agreed, these rights and responsibilities are
not affected and remain unchanged. Our Governments will continue,
as heretofore, to exercise supreme authority in the Western Sectors of
Berlin, within the framework of the Four Power responsibility which
we share for Berlin as a whole.

---

[4] Handed by the Ambassador of the U.S.S.R. to the three Ambassadors prior to
the signing of the agreement.

In accordance with Part II(A) of the Quadripartite Agreement, arrangements implementing and supplementing the provisions relating to civilian traffic will be agreed by the competent German authorities. Part III of the Quadripartite Agreement provides that the Agreement will enter into force on a date to be specified in a Final Quadripartite Protocol which will be concluded when the arrangements envisaged between the competent German authorities have been agreed. It is the request of our Governments that the envisaged negotiations now take place between authorities of the Federal Republic of Germany, also acting on behalf of the Senat, and authorities of the German Democratic Republic.

Part II(B) and (D) and Annexes II and IV of the Quadripartite Agreement relate to the relationship between the Western Sectors of Berlin and the Federal Republic. In this connection, the following are recalled inter alia:

> the communications of the three Western Military Governors to the Parliamentary Council of 2 March, 22 April and 12 May, 1949,

> the letter of the three High Commissioners to the Federal Chancellor concerning the exercise of the reserved Allied rights relating to Berlin of 26 May 1952 in the version of the letter X of 23 October 1954,

> the Aide Memoire of the three Governments of 18 April 1967 concerning the decision of the Federal Constitutional Court of 20 January 1966 in the Niekisch case.

Our Governments take this occasion to state, in exercise of the rights and responsibilities relating to Berlin, which they retained in Article 2 of the Convention on Relations between the Three Powers and the Federal Republic of Germany of 26 May 1952 as amended October 23, 1954, that Part II (B) and (D) and Annexes II and IV of the Quadripartite Agreement concerning the relationship between the Federal Republic of Germany and the Western Sectors of Berlin accord with the position in the above mentioned documents, which remains unchanged.

With regard to the existing ties between the Federal Republic and the Western Sectors of Berlin, it is the firm intention of our Governments that, as stated in Part II(B) (1) of the Quadripartite Agreement, these ties will be maintained and developed in accordance with the letter from the three High Commissioners to the Federal Chancellor on the exercise of the reserved rights relating to Berlin of 26 May 1952, in the version of letter X of October 23, 1954, and with pertinent decisions of the Allied Kommandatura of Berlin.

Accept, Excellency, the renewed assurance of our highest esteem. For the Government of the French Republic:

Jean Sauvagnargues.

For the Government of the United Kingdom of Great Britain and Northern Ireland:

Roger Jackling.

For the Government of the United States of America:

Kenneth Rush.

Communication From Allied Kommandatura to the Governing Mayor of Berlin

BKC/L(71)1 dated September 3

The Allied Kommandatura refers to the Quadripartite Agreement signed on September 3 in Berlin.

Part II (C) and Annex III, Paragraph 5, of the Quadripartite Agreement provide that arrangements implementing and supplementing the provisions relating to travel, communications and the exchange of territory will be agreed by the competent German authorities. Part IV of the Quadripartite Agreement provides that the Agreement will enter into force on a date to be specified in a Final Quadripartite Protocol which will be concluded when the arrangements envisaged between the competent German authorities have been agreed.

The Senat of Berlin is hereby authorized and requested to conduct appropriate negotiations on the subjects covered in Paragraphs 1, 2 and 3 in Annex III.

Draft Protocol on Entry Into Force [5]

Final Quadripartite Protocol

The Governments of the United States of America, the French Republic, the Union of Soviet Socialist Republics and the United Kingdom of Great Britain and Northern Ireland,

Having in mind Part III of the Quadripartite Agreement of September 3, 1971, and taking note with satisfaction of the fact that the agreements and arrangements mentioned below have been concluded,

---

[5] Initialed by the four Ambassadors on Sept. 3.

130

Have agreed on the following:

1. The four Governments, by virtue of this Protocol, bring into force the Quadripartite Agreement, which, like this Protocol, does not affect quadripartite agreements or decisions previously concluded or reached.

2. The four Governments proceed on the basis that the agreements and arrangements concluded between the competent German authorities (list of agreements and arrangements) shall enter into force simultaneously with the Quadripartite Agreement.

3. The Quadripartite Agreement and the consequent agreements and arrangements of the competent German authorities referred to in this Protocol settle important issues examined in the course of the negotiations and shall remain in force together.

4. In the event of a difficulty in the application of the Quadripartite Agreement or any of the above-mentioned agreements or arrangements which any of the four Governments consider serious, or in the event of non-implementation of any part thereof, that Government will have the right to draw the attention of the other three Governments to the provisions of the Quadripartite Agreement and this Protocol and to conduct the requisite quadripartite consultations in order to ensure the observance of the commitments undertaken and to bring the situation into conformity with the Quadripartite Agreement and this Protocol.

5. This Protocol enters into force on the date of signature.

Done at the building formerly occupied by the Allied Control Council in the American Sector of Berlin this _____ day of _____ 1971, in four originals, each in the English, French and Russian languages, all texts being equally authentic.

For the Government of the United States
of America:

For the Government of the French Republic:

For the Government of the Union of Soviet
Socialist Republics:

For the Government of the United Kingdom
of Great Britain and Northern Ireland:

Cover and book design: Pat Taylor